PROVEN WORD books have proven themselves where it counts — among the thousands of readers who have made them best-sellers because they found them meaningful in the arena of life.

These books were best-sellers in hardcover and are now offered at a more affordable price in deluxe paperback bindings.

These special editions also offer you a built-in study guide with insightful questions which will encourage group discussions as well as personal reflection and thought.

The *Proven Word* series addresses the widespread needs of people everywhere who are searching for the answers to the pressures and problems of living in today's modern world.

Disciplines
of the
Beautiful
Woman

Other books by Anne Ortlund:

Up with Worship
The Acts of Joanna
Discipling One Another
Children Are Wet Cement
Building a Great Marriage

with Ray C. Ortlund:

The Best Half of Life
Calm Down and Toughen Up

ANNE ORTLUND

Disciplines of the *Beautiful Woman*

WORD PUBLISHING

Dallas · London · Vancouver · Melbourne

Library of Congress Cataloging in Publication Data

Ortlund, Anne.
Disciplines of the beautiful woman.

1. Women—Conduct of life.   I. Title.
BJ1610.077   248'.843   77-76347
ISBN 0-8499-2983-0

Library of Congress Catalog Card Number: 77-76347

Scripture quotations marked TLB are from *The Living Bible, Paraphrased* (Wheaton: Tyndale House Publishers, 1971) and are used by permission. Quotations marked KJV are from the King James Version of the Bible. All other quotations are from *The New American Standard Bible,* copyright 1960, 1962, 1963, 1968, 1971 by the Lockman Foundation and used by permission.

Printed in the United States of America

5 6 7 8 9 LBM 29 28 27

To the three women I most admire
and who most influence me,
our two daughters and our daughter-in-law,
this book is affectionately dedicated:
Sherry Harrah
Margie McClure
Jani Ortlund

Contents

A. How This Book Got Started

The doctor leaned back. "There are lots of cysts in there," he said softly in an Alabama drawl. "You're gonna have to have surgery and get those out."

"Well," I said, "Something like ten years from now? I've got lots to do."

"Those cysts aren't gonna get any smaller," he said patiently.

I mentally shifted gears. "Okay, let's do it and I'll write a book." I could sense a delicious feeling coming over me.

"What does your schedule look like?" he asked.

We figured it out. Ray and I were leaving shortly for a Mediterranean cruise; after that I had a break from conference speaking because of Thanksgiving and Christmas.

"How about right after you get back?" he said.

"Give me a week," I said. "We always get our picture taken the first part of November for Christmas cards."

November 18, then.

So off we went across the Atlantic, with me blowing up balloons thirty times a day—that was to strengthen my lungs or something, I'm not sure what—in Israeli buses, aboard ship, in Grecian restaurants and Turkish spots of biblical interest. . . .

"Friends, this is where Paul heard the call, 'Come over to Macedonia and help us. . . .'"

Bang!

I left pieces of rubber all over the Middle East.

B. From the Hospital

This is November 20: two days past November 18, which was hysterectomy day for me. (For the last month, since surgery came into view, I've been wondering why "hysterectomy" and "hysterical" seem to have the same root word!)

Now at last my eyes are just beginning to focus; the mountains are beautiful out my window; my bed is rolled up into a sitting position, and I can once more put words on paper. A little. I'll pick at it.

Romans 12:1–2 is wonderful: "I present my body a living sacrifice." How silly to give God only my heart or my allegiance or whatever, and not my body! Certainly it is his to anesthetize, to roll into operating rooms, to poke with needles or fill with pills—to do all or none of these things, as he jolly-well pleases. He is my Lord. I am absolutely relaxed to let him do with my body what he wants.

The night before surgery, the last words I read were these: "May all God's mercies and peace be yours from God our Father and from Jesus Christ our Lord" (Rom 1:7, TLB). I thought about all God's mercies: his loving concern for me, his tenderly watching over me more efficiently even than doctors and machines and charts. I thought about his peace: the sense of well-being he gives, the cocoon-like feeling that his presence imparts. *Father, you're so wonderful. All things work together for good to those who love you.*

One of the disciplines of a godly woman must be the discipline of the mind. We are not free to let our emotions flip and flop all over the place. We are not free to fret and worry if we feel like it, to indulge ourselves in pouting and stewing. That doesn't mean that "blues" aren't permissible; they are. Many of the Psalms are David's laying out his feelings openly before the Lord—his "down" feelings as well as his "up" feelings—but putting them both into God's hands in completely surrendered faith. "Lord, I feel great today; I praise you"; or "Lord, I feel lousy today, but I praise you, anyway." Bad feelings aren't necessarily the result of sin; if I feel down, maybe I just ate something that didn't agree with me.

But *anxiety*—that's something else. Worry is disobedience. The disciplined mind makes no room for doubting God's plans for me. "What if———?" has no place in my thinking. The graph he has plotted for me can include automobile accidents, visits to the zoo, hot chocolate in front of the fire, hysterectomies—it's up to him.

A nurse has come in and given me a red and white Thing to blow into, something to protect my lungs from filling with fluid, so I'm holding it with my left hand and blowing while I write doggedly with my right. Now the nurse is discussing over my head the neighboring patient's needlepoint. I'll give up for now. . . .

. . . Quiet is a blessed gift. In this frantic world how we must cherish every moment of it, and carve it out for ourselves every chance we get. . . .

Before the interruption of the red and white Thing, Brother Lawrence was just about to come into my mind. He said we don't truly know peace in our hearts until pain is as welcome to us as lack of pain. Then the times when we feel no pain won't be marred by apprehension over the future when maybe we *will*. And pain is God's beautiful gift, anyway, to make us lean harder on him, when he knows we need it.

Or pain can simply be the means to that quiet we so long for. I had to laugh over a get-well card I received today:

It sure isn't easy,
Just 'resting' in bed [Are you kidding? It's gorgeous!]
When you'd much rather be
"Up and doing" instead. [Who, me?]
But relax, take it easy;
Think of all that you'll do
When you're up again, out again,
Feeling like new.

I could say facetiously, "Thanks for reminding me; you just ruined my whole day." No, really, I'm living a very full life right here in bed, two days after surgery. I'm practicing the presence of God; I'm enjoying thoughts of him and all his goodness; and when I'm "up again, out again," I trust my life will be just as full as it is right now—full of him.

God, discipline my mind before you. "Thou wilt keep him in perfect peace, whose mind is stayed on thee: because he trusteth in thee" (Isa. 26:3, KJV). May I relax and cuddle my feminine self in the pink fluffy stuff which is your will for me and my unquestioning obedience to you. Life has no other soft pillow but that! All else is steep precipices and darkness and sudden new violence. But in you, Lord—in your will, in your presence—*all is well.*

"Therefore my heart is glad, and my glory rejoiceth" and two days after surgery, "my flesh also shall rest in hope" (Ps. 16:9, KJV).

C. Shift from Me to You

There you are, a woman—how wonderful! How unique you are, not "made in Japan" but made in your mother's womb. A factory needs plenty of light; God was so smart he could make you perfectly in the dark.

That cowlick of yours, the length of your toes, your upper lip—he made all of you, and you are therefore very special and precious. (I'm unique, too. Children are amazed to see the crack right down the center of my tongue; I've never seen another tongue like it!)

The timing of your life is also unique. This is what Psalm 139 says: not only are *you* one-of-a-kind, but so is your life. Your particular birth-to-death span was planned by God 'way beforehand.

Have you become aware of a developing pattern in your personal life? Is there something inside of you like a time-release capsule; every so often does something softly explode within you; are new gifts released, or new interests, or new opportunities?

I'm praying this book will trigger in you a new gentle explosion—or maybe total revolution. Much of this material I've given in women's conferences, and then letters like these come in the mail:

Your talk meant more to me than any I had ever heard. . . . Since that time there have been so many radical changes I can hardly believe it myself.

I really feel one of those books you plan to write should be a combination of your own life experiences and 'how-to's'.

Well, my life, too, has been a series of time-releases:

At age six, the first explosion. My father and mother surrendered their lives to Jesus Christ, which totally affected their lives and all their children's. At the time Dad was a young Army lieutenant stationed at Fort Benning, Georgia. For the next forty years, including Dad's career as a general, he and Mother taught Bible classes on all the posts where they were ever assigned. Now they've been a year in heaven, but I'm still teaching Bible classes and loving God's Word.

Length of effect of time-release capsule: forever!

At age ten, explosion number two: bang! Mr. Resta, my piano teacher and a great influence in my life, started me writing music.

Effect so far: around 250 songs and pieces, some published and used.

At age twelve: poof! Mr. Addleman, another wise, good man, began teaching me pipe organ.

Effect: an organ major, Bachelor of Music degree, an Associate degree from the American Guild of Organists, and a dozen years as organist on the "Old-Fashioned Revival Hour" radio program.

At age twenty: pow! The Navy arrived at my university, and I met Ray Ortlund. Seventeen days after our first date, on 29 August 1944, I wrote this:

> How glad I am I came your way
> And got acquainted with you, Ray!
> These last few weeks have held such joy;
> I've never known a Christian boy
> Like you before. The Lord's been good
> —of course, just as I knew He would!—
> In time of deepest need, to send
> The fellowship of such a friend. . . .

[It was World War II, and my only brother and closest companion, Captain Robert E. Sweet, U.S.A.F., had just been killed when his plane went down. Life was lonely at that moment, deeply lonely—but campus life went on.]

> Our struggles over poli-sci
> (And even that's been fun with you!)
> The horseback ride—that lovely sky—
> The fun at Soltaus' barbecue,
> The picnic in the park, badminton
> Victories we never scored!—
> The concert at the Bowl, of course
> Our prayer group meetings with the Lord . . .
>   And then today you looked at me.—
>   And such a look! What did you see
>   Within my eyes that lit yours so
>   With such a sweet, disturbing glow?
>   Dear blue eyes, radiant Christian face,
>   It may be in the dear Lord's grace
>   That our two futures hold in store
>   Just that one look, and nothing more;
>   But oh, how sweet the memory
>   Of that one look will always be!
>   How glad I am I came your way
>   And got acquainted with you, Ray. . . .

Effect of time-release capsule: thirty-two years of close love, still increasing and bursting occasionally in new minireleases.

At age thirty-four: The baby-raising period was over; Sherry, Margie, and Bud were eleven, ten, and nine; and I began to be invited to speak here and there.

Continuing effect: lots of conference-speaking.

At age forty-six: pow! A personal spiritual renewal at the Wheaton College revival where Ray was speaker. Since then the fullness has begun to overflow in book-writing.

What other capsules are yet inside of me? I can hardly wait to know! I'm ready, Lord!

What's inside of you, a wonderful, unique woman made by God for very special reasons? He never wastes anything!

And this is the woman's day. Whoever you are—young, old, married, single, mother or not, working woman, housewife—you were never taken more seriously by your world. This is *your* day. I write this book to help you see where you've come from and where you are, to cut away the unnecessary, to release one of God's time-capsules within you.

Several capsules?

1. *Your First Decision, and What Follows*

The great majority of women in this world, not understanding that God has specific plans for their lives, would tell you that they just "take life as it comes." Because their lives have only a horizontal, humanistic dimension, they'd readily agree that they "just live one day at a time." Actually, that's what's known as drifting down the lazy ol' river, man, and it feels so good. . . .

Only it ends up at Niagara Falls.

Oh, my friend, I don't know you, but you're a little bit precious to me because you're reading my book (!), and you're very precious to God because he made you. Maybe these next words don't apply to you at all (I pray they don't!), but consider them, just in case, with all your heart.

Where are you in your life? Upstream, barely aware of the tugging current, thinking you're getting along all right on your own? Or maybe being carried rapidly along, occasionally realizing that you're not in control, but not knowing what to do about it? Or with the roar of disaster in your ears, unable to cope with your anguish and despair?

In any of these cases, listen so carefully. Niagara Falls is described in God's Word like this: "It is appointed for men to die once, and after this comes judgment" (Heb. 9:27).

But at any point in your life, including right now, God's hand is extended tenderly and strongly to lift you out of the canoe and onto solid ground. All you have to do is reach out to him! This is known in the Bible as "salvation," and whether it sounds old-fashioned or not, every living person needs to be saved.

The Apostle Peter told about it like this to some people who needed to be saved:

> You no doubt know that Jesus of Nazareth was anointed by God with the Holy Spirit and with power, and he went around doing good and healing all who were possessed by demons, for God was with him.
>
> And we apostles are witnesses of all he did throughout Israel and in Jerusalem, where he was murdered on a cross. But God brought him back to life again three days later. . . . And he sent us to preach the Good News everywhere and to testify that Jesus is ordained of God to be the Judge of all—living and dead. And all the prophets have written about him, saying that everyone who believes in him will have their sins forgiven through his Name (Acts 10:38–43, TLB).

One way or another, you have probably heard that story before, but right now take a fresh look at it. (Who knows, maybe your canoe trip is about over.) There are three elements to the story:

1. Jesus died on a cross and rose again the third day from the dead.
2. God has ordained him to be the future judge of all. (That's the Niagara Falls trip for those who don't heed his warning.)
3. Anyone who opens his eyes to the situation is free to reach for his hand: to believe in Jesus Christ and be forgiven of all sins, through the power of his wonderful name.

That's truly simple, isn't it? But if it's that simple, why does anyone hesitate? Because, my friend, it means giving up the canoe! The woman who reaches for Jesus Christ to save her has to disassociate her heart from that picnic lunch and the Saks-Fifth hand-knit sweater and her purse and binoculars and the portable TV—and many hesitate, gripped by paralysis!

But see the situation from a helicopter—from God's point of view, in the light of eternity. What shall it profit if you gain the whole canoe (for a short while) and lose your own soul— forever? While there's still time, reach out your hand to his.

I'm typing with tears in my eyes. Do stop reading, please; let him urge you, himself, and reach for him right now.

Let's presume (and I pray it's really true) that all of us now, I writing and you reading, are safely on the bank. Here's where "cream puff religion"—no strain, no pain—has deceived many, leading new Christians to believe that once they're out of the canoe onto land, they're in heaven! So a few months later when they still have problems, they're disillusioned.

Actually this is the time when we brush ourselves off, set our eyes on that distant City, and start walking. Cross country, woman. Realize what you were saved from, and know that that place is so fabulous it's worth hiking over hills, through thorns, through rivers up to our lipstick, over cliffs—anything to get there. I pray I'll motivate you up to the point of delirious exhaustion, because that City is worth getting to.

Yes, this is a book about the *disciplines* of getting to Christian maturity. There's a great difference between opening our eyes to danger and being helped out of a canoe (just a simple, sensible act) and the subsequent slogging over miles of life, one step at a time, one decision at a time in choosing our course, suffering anything, and arriving gloriously at our destination.

Now, the amazing thing is that if we're willing to do this we won't end up exhausted old frumps in muddy hiking boots. Through the tears, pain, and fatigue we'll grow into God's beautiful women. We'll arrive at the City with better posture, and looking zingier and lovelier, than when we began.

And the most wonderful part of all, the part that makes the whole process a worthy prelude to heaven, is the discovery that the hand that lifted us out of the canoe will never, never let go. By destination time we will know the warm clasp of those fingers very well, and it would be unthinkable not to be unceasingly conscious of his grip.

So we press on—and press on—and press on! Dear friend, there are so many in this world who are eager-beaver starters, and so few who are glorious finishers! The one thing I fear is that after I've encouraged other women toward Christ I'll stumble myself and fall on my face. I don't want to, oh, I really don't.

But when the Apostle Paul was an "old pro" as a Christian he wrote, "I haven't learned all I should even yet, but I keep working toward that day when I will finally be all that Christ saved me for and wants me to be. No, dear brothers, I am still not all I should be but I am bringing all my energies to bear on this one thing" (Phil. 3:12, 13, TLB).

I came to know the Lord in a Christian home as a little girl, was raised in a great combination of strictness and fun, somehow missed rebelliousness in the teen years, grew up hoping I'd marry a minister and did, raised Christian kids and taught Bible classes and dearly loved the whole local church scene. But after I'd been a pastor's wife maybe twenty years, J began to get thirstier and thirstier for more of God in my life.

I didn't understand what it was I wanted. One time when I'd read Ephesians 3:19, "That you might be filled up to all the fullness of God," I wrote in the margin of my Bible, "How can you put the ocean in a teacup?" What you haven't experienced, you never understand.

I would underline verses like "As the deer pants for water,

so I long for You, O God. I thirst for God, the living God. Where can I find him to come and stand before him?" (Ps. 42:1, TLB). And "O God, my God! How I search for you! How I thirst for you in this parched and weary land where there is no water. How I long to find you!" (Ps. 63:1, TLB).

Pretty soon I was absolutely cotton-mouthed.

Ray felt the same—and he was the respected, faithful pastor of a large church. I remember his saying to me at the time, "Anne, you've got to pray for me! I'm so undisciplined! I've got to cut out extra meetings, prune and trim, and give myself more time to get deep in God's Word. I long to be closer to Christ, and I know it takes time. But I want more of Jesus!"

In that same period of time, which was building around our lives the way those wonderful beach waves build around your body before they crest, twenty-one-year-old Bud happened to be home from college. I was about to speak somewhere and I said, "What shall I say, Bud?"

He said, "Mother, tell them only Jesus satisfies—not a suburban house, not color TV, not a station wagon and a sexy wife. No trip satisfies, only the Lord."

Then he spread out his hands on the table before me and said, "That's what I want. The way the planets revolve around the sun, I want my life to revolve around him. I want him absolutely central."

I can remember looking out the window, and thinking how Sherry and Margie, our two collegian daughters, felt exactly the way Bud felt. And I remembered Isaiah 44: "I will give you abundant water for your thirst and for your parched fields. And I will pour out my Spirit and my blessings on your children. They shall thrive like watered grass, like willows on a river bank. 'I am the Lord's, they'll proudly say" (Isa. 44:3–5, TLB).

It's six years later, the six best years yet for Ray and me. The Lord has truly overflowed in all our lives. The three older children are all in the ministry, and our little eleven-year-old adopted tadpole-son, Nels, is coming along fine in his own happy-go-lucky way.

What have I learned in these last six years? That Spirit-motivated *disciplines* facilitate the Christian walk. Oh, I'm not discounting all the warm feelings along the route, when I've sung Jesus-songs and held hands and the rest. But our sensuous age forgets that feelings come and feelings leave you, but the disciplines of life are what get you to where you want to go.

Do you feel as if your life is like a jammed closet, and you keep muttering now and then, "Some day I'm going to get organized"? Well, I'm not all the way there yet, but let me share with you what I've learned—woman to woman.

2. Reshaping Your Life to Three Priorities

When a sculptor starts to shape a human form from a huge lump of clay, he doesn't detail the eyes and cheekbones first. He works with the large masses, attempts to get the head proportioned to the body, to set the direction of the trunk, and so on.

As you consider your whole lifestyle, you've got to think about what your top priorities are going to be, before you decide what time you're going to get up in the morning. Let's deal with the large mass of your life first, and I want to suggest to you three priorities that can't be circumvented,[1] though they may gouge and rudely disfigure your present life-form before you get things rearranged.

God first!

You're criticizing me. I can feel it: "Too vague, too theoretical." "HODE IT, HODE IT," as our Nels says. (That's a carryover from baby talk and it's now a family expression.) Wait a minute; don't prejudge.

---

[1] See Raymond C. Ortlund, *Lord, Make My Life a Miracle!* (Glendale, Cal.: Regal Books, 1975).

"Seek first His kingdom and His righteousness, and all these [other] things shall be added to you" says the Bible (Matt. 6:33). We're to be seekers after Jesus, first. Everything else must flow out of the first. And really first! Top of the list in our lives! "The old saying of 'putting first things first' is not quite good enough. The New Testament makes it evident that the 'first' of which it speaks is a singular and not a plural; 'putting the first *thing* first' would be the only proper statement of the matter. . . . Anything else that might be taken out of 'all the rest' and set up as 'first' inevitably will result in doublemindedness rather than a single focus." [2]

Don't think of yourself first as a wife or a single person or a mother or a worker in some field; you will some day stand before God all by yourself.

Says Proverbs 9:12, "If you are wise, you are wise for yourself, and if you scoff, you alone will bear it." Shed all relationships, all functions from your thinking, and consider yourself first as a woman. What will God have you be and do? He will not say at the Judgment, "I excuse you from this or that because your husband didn't cooperate," or "I understand that you didn't have time to know my Word because of your job. . . ." No one, nothing must keep you from putting God first in your life. You would have all eternity to be sorry.

We must all know intellectually and experientially that God is first. He must be our lives—in a class all by himself. Everything in our lives must converge at that one point: Christ. That's the only way we'll become integrated, focused, whole women. Jesus said, "Any kingdom divided against itself is laid waste; and any city or house divided against itself shall not stand" (Matt. 12:25). Are you divided against yourself?

The words of an anthem I wrote say it this way:

---

[2] Vernard Eller, *The Simple Life* (Grand Rapids, Mich.: Eerdmans Pub. Co., 1973), p. 21.

How single, God, are You—how whole!
One Source are You, one Way, one Goal.
I tend to splinter all apart
With fractured mind, divided heart;
Oh, integrate my wand'ring maze
To one highway of love and praise.

O single, mast'ring Life of peace
At Whose command the ragings cease,
Keep calling to me "Peace, be still,"
To redirect my scattered will.
Keep gath'ring back my heart to You.
Keep cent'ring all I am and do.

O focused Spot of holy ground,
Silence which is the Source of sound,
I drop the clutter from my soul,
Reorganized by Your control;
Then single, whole, before Your throne,
I give myself to You alone.[3]

I've been learning that functioning as a pastor's wife, as *Ray's* wife, or speaking, teaching, composing, writing, mothering—none of the good things in my life dare be a substitute for the best. God can have no competition in your heart, or in mine.

Are you saying, "I'm really afraid of total surrender; I've got so many dreams and plans, and I'm not sure what would happen to them if I give myself totally to God"?

The first Queen Elizabeth asked a man to go abroad for her on business.

"I sincerely wish I could, but I can't," said the man. "My business is very demanding. It would really suffer if I left."

"Sir," replied the Queen, "if you will attend to *my* business, I will take care of *your* business."

---

[3] © Copyright 1976 Anne Ortlund. All rights reserved.

Work out the implications in your own life of putting God first. That's what this book is to help you do.

If we feel overworked and someone tells us to take a rest— that's temporary. If he tells us to go on a vacation, we'll come back afterward to the same old rat race. If he tells us to go to God, we've found a permanent solution. We'll be revolutionized. We'll go into our work rested, and remain that way.

"My presence shall go with you," God says, "and I will give you rest" (Exod. 33:14).

Let your heart go to God, then! Go to him, never to go elsewhere again. Settle into him; make him your home. John 15 calls it "abiding" in him—to nestle there, secure as in a strong, eternal fortress.

We were coming home after living for three months in Afghanistan, and in a Vienna hotel I put this idea into poetry:

From here to there, and then from there to here
The people of this planet circling roam,
And I, as well—but, oh, one truth is clear:
I live in God, and God Himself is Home.

From hither and from thither comes the call,
Perhaps to places near, perhaps abroad,
But anywhere I am, and through it all
My heart's at home—for Home is Sovereign God.

To hurry here, and then to scurry there
May be the thing that duty asks of me;
But oh! my heart is tranquil anywhere,
When God Himself is my Tranquility.

Yes, in my heart of heart Shekinah dwells—
The Glorious One, the Highest and the Best;
And deep within, I hear cathedral bells
That call me to devotion and to rest.[4]

---

[4] © Copyright 1972 Anne Ortlund. Used by permission.

Dear Christian sister, do we just know God? Or do we really *know* him? The Apostle Paul, a veteran super-Christian, wrote in Philippians 3:8-10, "I count all things to be loss in view of the surpassing value of knowing Christ Jesus my Lord, for whom I have suffered the loss of all things, and count them but rubbish in order . . . that I may know Him, and the power of His resurrection." What did he mean? Let me give you Ray's explanation taken from an unedited tape just the rough, beautiful way Ray preaches, in pure Rayortlundese:

> . . . That I may know Him, and the power of His resurrection. . . ." Now, we *must* know facts *about* God, but then we must go on—go on, my friend, to the great discovery of God himself, God himself. You see, Paul was a veteran in the faith. He was in jail for Jesus' sake. And yet he pleads that he may know God.
>
> Friend, you were built to know God; and as you know him, and you get to know him as God himself, God himself—you come upon an ecstasy for which you were made. The facts *about* God are important. But God himself, to move into God is that for which you have been constructed.
>
> "Get to know God!" Paul cried out!

In our first little church in rural Pennsylvania was a very old woman, the oldest person we had ever seen. Miss Ettie Neal was ninety-seven, and she was permanently in bed from a broken hip. The first time a church elder took her new blond twenty-six-year-old pastor to see her, she looked up and squeaked, "Oh, my! He's just a boy!" And truly, to her he was.

But every week Ray would go to visit Miss Ettie, and he would sit by her bed and take her bony hand in his (when she's 97 and the guy's 26, it's all right), and he would read the Bible and pray with her.

One day—now, think of this—Miss Ettie told Ray that when she was a little girl she'd gone to Washington, D.C., and had shaken hands with President Abraham Lincoln! Maybe some of you readers want to look up my husband and shake the hand that shook the hand that shook the hand. . . .

Now, if someone from, say, Burma, said to me, "Do you know Abraham Lincoln?" I would say, "Certainly! He was one of our American presidents, at the time of our Civil War," and so on. But I don't know Abraham Lincoln as did Miss Ettie Neal.

And Miss Ettie didn't know Abraham Lincoln as did young Tad Lincoln, who could burst through his White House study doors any time, and climb up on those bony knees and be the recipient of his wisdom and love.

Do you see what I mean? We can know God, or we can come to *know God,* and it makes all the difference in the world. If you set yourself to really come to know him, you'll be a rare person indeed. This is what separates the winners from the fool-around-ers: setting your face toward truly making God the number one priority of your life.

How do we do this? Let me suggest four ways; his Spirit will teach you many more.

First, practice his presence. Jesus did! He said, "Do you not believe that I am in the Father, and the Father is in Me?" (John 14:10). Yes, Jesus was special; he was part of the Trinity; but he tells us also to abide in him! So we get our clues from Jesus: when we abide continually in the Father, the words that we speak won't be spoken on our own initiative; the Father within us will do the works.

Live your life consciously before him, moment by moment. Trust him to help you do it. Psalm 16:8 says, "I have set the Lord continually before me; because He is at my right hand, I will not be shaken."

Second, jealously guard a daily quiet time spent alone with God. Jesus did! He sent the multitudes away—and prayed (Matt. 14:23). When our three babies were age 2½, 1½, and brand new, I found my days were just one succession of bottles and diapers, and I got desperate for times with the Lord! Normally I sleep like a rock, but I said, "Lord, if you'll help me, I'll meet you from two to three A.M." I kept my tryst with him until the schedule lightened; I didn't die; and I'm not sorry I did it. Everybody has twenty-four hours. We can soak ourselves in prayer, in his Word, in himself, if we really want to.

Third, seek the Lord in occasional longer hunks of time. Jesus did! In Luke 6:12 he spent an entire night in prayer, because he felt the need—he, the Son of God! How much more do we need these extended times with God? Ray and I take one day a month, usually, to go out of town and pray, think, check our schedules, evaluate where we've been, see where we're going, discuss how we're doing as a wife, as a husband. The time is all too short!

And fourth, be diligent in your attendance of public worship.[5] Jesus was! Luke 4:16 says that *"as was His custom, He entered the synagogue on the Sabbath"* (emphasis mine). Certainly the Son of God wasn't going to church "for what he would get out of it." Maybe it was often less than the best. He went because he pleased the Father in all things. Be committed to public worship of God every week whether you feel like it or not, whether the preaching is great or isn't! We go for what *God* gets out of it. He wants us to be there, not via television or radio, but personally with the Body of Christ (Heb. 10:25).

The second highest priority of your life must be commitment to this very Body. That's one reason why you must never fail to worship with them. Your physical family is precious, but they are temporary—for this world only. Your spiritual family is eternal. There is much we haven't learned yet about how to function as spiritual fathers and mothers, brothers and sisters, single aunts and uncles, and daughters and sons, and we're the poorer for it. This doesn't put down that pre-

---

[5] See Anne Ortlund, *Up with Worship* (Glendale, Cal.: Regal Books, 1975).

cious, unique physical family of yours; it simply raises in your thinking the level of the spiritual family! A deep prayer life with, and accountability to, some close members of the spiritual family can help make your relationship with your physical family what it ought to be.

There's a lot of talk these days which pits the church against the family—a cruel thing to do, like trying to make two friends into enemies. This kind of talk makes the church the spanking boy every time, implying that it's "spiritual" to refuse to usher, sing in the choir or teach a Sunday School class, so that we can sit home with our families in front of the television with our feet up and munch corn chips.

There is dangerous, twisted thinking here. Let me tell you about my friend Bruce's family of schnauzers. We paid a visit when mamma schnauzer had her puppies. The whole family of them were in a playpen in the kitchen. That enclosure was their whole world, and those tiny pups snuggled to their mother for warmth, food, love—everything they needed.

They had no idea that they were totally dependent on a larger family, a human family—Bruce and June and their children—who were (under God) the ultimate source of the provision of all their needs.

Do you have a physical family? Then snuggle close together and enjoy the warmth, food, and love hopefully provided there. But recognize that your true source of godly love, warmth, nourishment, and togetherness should come from the larger family, the eternal family. Look carefully at the emphasis of the New Testament epistles, God's directions for us in this church age. They tell us to use our gifts to nourish the Body of Christ, and draw our nourishment from the Body, so that all the adult singles, young people without Christian parents, and marrieds without Christian spouses will feel just as cared for and loved and nourished as anyone else in God's beautiful forever-family. And when we're loved and fed and prayed for there, our lacks and needs in our physical family relationships will be wonderfully met.

Paul knew what it was to hold the family of God the highest of all human relationships. He wrote to the Philippians, "It is only right for me to feel this way about you all, because I have you in my heart. . . . God is my witness, how I long for you all with the affection of Christ Jesus. And this I pray, that your love may abound still more and more." (Phil. 1:7–9).

"Oh, boy!" we think. "Those Philippians must have been so lovable, so adorable, so wonderful—not like the Christians in *my* church!" Then we get over to chapter four and find that Euodia and Syntyche were fighting. These were good women, who were both workers for the Lord, and Paul pled with the church to find some go-between to reconcile them and keep the church from splitting apart.

Yes, the early Christians were just like us latter Christians, with all the same temptations and weaknesses, and if we're going to love each other with a true "Priority Two" kind of love, it means struggling over a threshold of pain to get there.

Gilbert Tennent was pastor of a Presbyterian church in Philadelphia around 1750, and he had the fun of pastoring a church made up almost entirely of spiritual babies saved during the "Great Awakening," a spiritual revival that swept the American colonies in the middle of the century. One of his sermons was called "Brotherly Love Recommended by the Argument of the Love of God." (We'd never title a sermon that now, because it wouldn't fit on our bulletin boards.) But Tennent knew that the need of new Christians—all Christians—is to love each other. Here's what he told them, not in 1750 Philadelphia talk which we wouldn't understand too well, but a Ray Ortlund paraphrase—again rough, unedited, right off the tape:

He urged his congregation to love each other, and love each

other to the end. He said that when you begin to love each other, you come at a certain place—oh, hear me, my friends—you come at a certain place when you discover the real truth.

And in every one of our lives there's a can of worms. Believe you me! There's a skeleton in the closet of every life here. And you see, we can be known, or we can be willing to know, up to that point. That's it. That's safe—but that's superficial. But, he says, you must love right in through that painful area, right in through that painful point, love right on to the end. Refuse to let go, though you know everything about that person. Refuse to let go. He says fragile love will love up to a point—and that's not worth anything. That's what most Christians experience. But there are those who are willing to know and willing to be known, to the point where they go crashing right on through that threshold of pain, to where they really know and are known.

That, my friend—not a cup of coffee—is real Christian fellowship. Whatever church God has guided you to, whoever your Christian family is, get your heart together with theirs! Guard your unity! Attend to them, love them, care for them! Help them, strengthen them in God, teach them, be taught by them. And every time you're confronted by an area of painful difference, crash through!

Judy and I were in a small group of four together—meeting weekly, praying over the phone several times a week, being committed to each other at close range. Judy and I had a difference, and I guess we knew that sometime it would have to surface: Judy speaks in tongues, and I don't.

It came out one day while I was having lunch at her house, just the two of us. It became a two-hour lunch, with voices raised and interruptions—there was probably more heat than light! Bible pages were flipped and verses stabbed at, both of us trying to make our points. Finally we were hugging each other and crying, reiterating our commitment to each other through it all. And since that luncheon, there's been as much tension between Judy and me over our differing spiritual gifts, as between two sisters in a home where one has the gift of cooking and the other prefers to sew.[6]

The third priority of our lives, after God and his people, must be the needy people of our world. We musn't turn them off! A "God-bless-us-four-no-more" kind of life will soon make us introverted and provincial. The beautiful woman of Proverbs 31 "extends her hand to the poor; and she stretches out her hands to the needy" (v. 20).

Most people admire philanthropy, missions, and witnessing —but they leave them to the super people on whom they look with not a little awe and reverence. That's ridiculous! There are people all around us in deep trouble and desperately floundering, and they would welcome us as angels if we lent them some money, told them about Jesus, or met whatever their need happens to be.

We know this, then why don't we act? Because if you're like me, I'm naturally—well, "chicken" is the word. I need a group of Christians to whom I'm regularly accountable, to whom I can lay out the needs of those around me, and who will be responsible for seeing that I act.

One day in the beauty parlor I sat down as usual under the hair dryer and was approached by a cute redhead.

"Hi," she said, "I'm Barbara. Your manicurist quit last week, and I'm taking over her patrons."

"Hello, Barbara," I said, and five minutes later she was sharing that her husband had left her, that she was afraid of being at home alone at night, that the children all thought it was her fault and not his—soon tears were falling all over my nail polish.

"Barbara," I said, "do you go to church?"

"No," she said. "And if I don't get my head together soon something terrible is going to happen."

"Would you go with me next Sunday?"

"Of course!"

---

[6] For more on relationships with fellow believers, see chapter 13.

I screwed up my courage. "Would you go to an adult Sunday School class, too?"

"Sure," she said, "I'll do anything!"

This was so easy, I decided to shoot the works.

"Barbara," I said, "if you really want the whole treatment, you need to do a third thing, too."

"Whatever you say," said Barbara.

"Well, you need to go to Sunday School, and you need to go to church, and then afterward you need to just hang around!"

Do you know all the wonderful things that can happen to the churchgoers who hang around afterward? The ones who bolt for the parking lot miss half the goodies. I'm thankful for my heritage of being raised by parents who were the last to leave the church, Sunday morning and Sunday evening! Even a newcomer can find her way into the hearts of the people if she'll hang around!

Through the weeks Barbara followed the one-two-three formula, and there was also an invisible foundation being laid under what was happening that she knew nothing about. Every week my group of sisters would ask, "What can we pray for, for Barbara? What's happening in your relationship with her? Are you having effective conversations with her about the Lord?" And then they'd pray—with me and for me.

Well, that kind of prodding from the rear is what any Christian needs who doesn't naturally have the gift of evangelism. And so it wasn't surprising that several months later, sitting beside me in church, Barbara confessed her faith in Jesus Christ as her Savior. (Ya-hoo! Three cheers! Fireworks in heaven!)

But do you see how the three priorities must be in that order, and then how they flow into each other? Priority One must come before Priority Two. Unless we are rich in God and in his Word, our spiritual lives will be thin and we will have nothing of eternal significance to contribute to our fellow Christians. And Priority Two must come before Priority

Three. Unless we are close in with our fellow Christians, the chances are we'll have little or no success in effectively reaching our world around us—maybe even our own families—for Christ.

The three priorities are such a practical part of my life now that they even affect my daily list of things to do. Often I come to a point in the day when I have choices: what's most important of the things left to be done?

I check off Priority One: have I had my daily time with God? No? Then that's next; everything else can wait. At the very least, it calls me back to an awareness of him.

I check off Priority Two: which of the remaining items on the list affect my brothers and sisters in Christ? I do them next.

I check off Priority Three. What of these items concerns my work in this world, my witness to it? They come next.

If I'm guided in my "to do" list by these three priorities, then the important takes precedence over the urgent. That's so necessary! If we live always doing the urgent, we spend our time responding to alarm bells and racing to put out fires. Ten years later we'll feel totally impoverished, because over the long haul the seemingly urgent is seldom important.

Take a good look at your life. Whatever kind of woman you are—wife, mother, career woman, single parent—have you got your priorities in order? Are you building a life of eternal consequences?

If not, like a good sculptor, you need to do some strong, radical gouging and reshaping to start making the large mass of your remaining life what you—and God—want it to be.

3. *Your Attitude toward Work*

You wouldn't believe where I'm writing these words.

"Try me," you say.

All right. I'm sitting on a puffy plum and purple couch in a nook of the Royal Hawaiian Hotel in Honolulu. To my right is a huge brass bowl of pink double hibiscus and purple orchids in giant star-bursts—the total arrangement a breathtaking fifteen feet tall and twelve feet wide. In front of me, beyond the magenta Monarch Room, I see an outrigger canoe mounting the waves of Waikiki. The sounds: surf, giggling swimmers, birdsong, quiet talk.

Ray and Nels and I are here in Hawaii for a month. We've done the sight-seeing before; this time we're in one spot, being quiet—reading, resting, praying, writing, playing.

"What a life," you say.

Indeed. What a life! But this month in Hawaii comes after work to the point of physical exhaustion.

It's been six months since surgery. The first two months I really rested and slept! But somehow, in the four months following, I've been speaker for nine Bible conferences, taught twenty-five Bible classes and had some other single speaking dates, written ten hymns and anthems, worked on this book, counseled, run the home and entertained for Jesus' sake, gone to church meetings; I've mothered Nels, played with Ray, and traveled from Los Angeles to Washington, D.C., San Francisco, Chicago, Birmingham, and San Diego. Two weeks ago I had a checkup, and my weight had slid down two more pounds.

"You're abusing your body," said Dr. Stewart.

(I must say I'd never thought of it. What I'd done I've been Spirit-gifted to do, which made it joyous work.)

But God is so kind! At that point he'd arranged a month of dead stop in Hawaii. This first week we've slept ten or more hours a day, and the pounds are going back on. . . .

I think of Paul's life:

"Are they servants of Christ?" he wrote of others, "I more so; in far more labors, in far more imprisonments, beaten times without number, often in danger of death" (2 Cor. 11:23).

"Where was Paul's Hawaii?" I ask myself. And he comforted the Hebrews, "You have not yet resisted to the point of shedding blood" (Heb. 12:4)—as Paul himself had.

Never do we see in the Bible the notion of "Now, be careful; don't overdo; take it easy." Somehow you and I do that very easily without being told.

But God puts a high level of value on work—all work, and especially eternal work: "Therefore, my beloved brethren, be steadfast, immovable, always abounding in the work of the Lord, knowing that your toil is not in vain in the Lord" (1 Cor. 15:58).

Payday is coming! What is the labor of this little life by comparison? Remember the example of Epaphroditus! Paul wrote about him to the Philippians: "Receive him in the Lord with all joy, and hold men like him in high regard; because he came close to death for the work of Christ, risking his life to complete what was deficient in your service to me" (Phil. 2:29–30).

There is no hint here that Paul ever rebuked him or tried to get him to slow down; there's nothing but commendation!

Obviously he was doing high-quality work; I want to make sure that my so-called Christian work isn't just shuffling papers, more or less. But to spend your precious years connecting people with God, influencing them toward heaven by every means we can think of—for this, my friend, don't mind getting totally, gloriously exhausted. We have only a few short years to earn our rewards, and then all eternity to enjoy them.

Let's think about so-called secular work.

You may be a single working woman—like Lydia, a dealer in expensive fabrics (Acts 16:14–15). Or you may be a working wife—like Priscilla, who made tents with her husband (Acts 18:2–3). Or you may preside over the running of a home —like Mary, John Mark's mother (Acts 12:12). All three became spiritually powerful women, and all three were certainly in God's will in their chosen vocations.

But I hope you work, one way or another, and God has plenty to say about work. There are twenty-eight Proverbs on the glory or the benefits of hard work! Interestingly enough, many couple it with having money; some don't. But consider these:

Lazy men are soon poor; hard workers get rich (Prov. 10:4, TLB).

Work hard and become a leader; be lazy and never succeed (Prov. 12:24, TLB).

Lazy people want much but get little, while the diligent are prospering (Prov. 13:4, TLB).

If you won't plow in the cold, you won't eat in the harvest (Prov. 20:4, TLB).

The lazy man is full of excuses. "I can't go to work," he says.

"If I go outside I might meet a lion in the street and be killed!" (Prov. 22:13, TLB).

Here's one that Solomon didn't write down, but could have: "The industrious spider gets a large web."

Hard work never hurt anybody. It's only a bad attitude toward work that causes the gears to grind, the tensions to mount. That's why our work done in God's will should only bring physical fatigue—from which rest will bounce us back —but not emotional or spiritual fatigue.

The world's supposedly oldest person, a Russian Caucasian man whose unproved age was 168, died recently. This fellow, Sirali Mislimdv, attributed his long life to constant work, mountain air, and moderate eating! According to the *Los Angeles Times* he chopped wood regularly, and on his last birthday worked all day in his garden, besides taking his usual half-mile walk.

The point is to see that work is God's plan for you. If you're exhausted emotionally and/or spiritually, check these points:

1. Have you rearranged your life to make God first—living in his presence and allowing plenty of time for worship, thanksgiving, his Word, and asking him about things?
2. Have you settled into the best church available, and made your fellow believers second in your life? Are you especially loving a few of them at such close range, in a "small group," so that you can exchange your joys and burdens and needs, get counsel from them, and be held accountable to them?
3. Have you a plan for reaching those around you for Christ? Are you giving yourself away to the physical and spiritual needs of others?

These three priorities, in this order, will probably give you all the spiritual and emotional stamina you need. But if you say "yes" to these three and your job still exhausts you, you may be in the wrong job.

Work is God's plan for us, so we must find the work that best suits our gifts. We will probably shift in our lives from one type of work to another; that's good. Circumstances may cause this, or maybe those time-capsules going off inside, opening up new interests and gifts.

But don't necessarily connect work and money! If you live on an inheritance or are supported by a husband, you still need to work without pay. The world is so needy! Give yourself away. Or maybe you have no income, and you still feel called to work without salary. Fine!

The source of your money is never your job. If it were and you lost your job, you might have a nervous collapse. No, the source of your money is God. He owns it all; he distributes it as he pleases; and he has promised over and over to take care of the physical needs of every one of his children.

I know a fellow who felt that God was calling him to go to seminary full time to be trained for the ministry. But he has a wife and two small children. He didn't see how he could go to school full time and minister to his family and work at a job as well; neither did he feel his wife should leave the children and go to work. School and family were higher priorities than a job, so he simply trusted God as his source of supply and started in to school. Through a continuous series of unexpected supplies, he's finished his first year of seminary with his needs cared for, and no debts.

God is always our source! Now, from tending the garden of Eden on, people have always been given important, meaningful things to do in life. These things are his will for us, and they may or may not cover our physical needs in reimbursement. Never mind. We're still to do them with all our hearts. Even Jesus said, "My food is to do the will of Him Who sent Me" (John 4:34)—and his own needs in turn were met.

But the life of faith demands that we *do his will first*—before we concern ourselves with supply. That is, before we concern ourselves with supply of money, physical energy, time, or any other need. In the Christian life it's not "seeing is believing"; it's "believing is seeing." *First* seek "His kingdom, and His righteousness," and *after that* "all these things shall be added to you" (Matt. 6:33).

In July of 1975 I got a real test of my willingness to do his will and expect him to supply time for me. What I'm talking about is not saying "yes" to every good thing that comes along; the overwilling person soon becomes the goat! Sometimes I've been that—although my more natural tendency is to be lazy. But this time God seemed to have legitimately called me to do more things than I had time to do.

I was up to my ears in writing, speaking, church work, counseling, composing, mothering, being available to Ray —and our church went into the "Evangelism Explosion" program.

"Anne," Ray said to me, "I'd really like you to get in on the ground floor of this to make sure it fits our church philosophy."

E.E. is a wonderful program, but it's a lot of hours every week of memorizing, visitation, and so on. I began to feel that the top of my head was ready to pop, but Ray had asked me—my loving, caring Ray—so I said yes. I wasn't sure how I'd manage it.

With the first week of the program came the news that our church organist was resigning. Whenever I'm needed I always fill in—and practicing for services is an extra seven hours a week, minimum. Suddenly I thought my head was going to pop for sure.

But almost immediately a lady emerged out of nowhere who said to me, "Anne, I would think that you must be a very busy person. I'd count it a privilege if you'd let me finance a part-time maid for you. How many hours could you use one?"

By the following week—and ever since—a dear woman,

conscientious and capable, has worked for me four half-days a week—shopping, running errands, cleaning and cooking, washing and ironing. She prays for me as she does it; she knows she's contributing to ministry; she brings me cups of tea or an encouraging word. The house shines, and my work load is exactly matched to my capacity. "Come to Me," says Jesus, "all who are weary and heavy laden, and I will give you rest. Take My yoke upon you and learn from Me, for I am gentle and humble in heart; and you shall find rest for your souls. For My yoke is easy, and My load is light" (Matt. 11:28–30).

Don't think the moral of this story is that every woman who serves Christ gets a trip to Hawaii and a maid. I only know that when we work in obedience to him, saying yes unreservedly before we see how, he will make it right. He will make it up to us in a thousand secret, delightful ways.

And we will learn to rest as we work. We will feel exhilarated, challenged, pushed along by the work he has given us to do.

Some have called this "The Age of the Great Goof-Off," when people want more and more money for less and less work. Dear Christian woman, see the glory of productivity. May part of the way you represent Christ in this world be your reputation for hard work!

"Walk in a manner worthy of the Lord," says Colossians 1:10, "to please Him in all respects, bearing fruit in every good work and increasing in the knowledge of God."

4. *Your Looks*

God forbid that anybody but my husband should see me the way I look when I first get out of bed. (He loves me very much.) Some women are just naturally gorgeous. Our daughter-in-law Jani is as beautiful when she steps out of the Pacific Ocean surf as when she steps out of her house for an evening date. Nels says it's because she's part Indian.

But me? For one thing, I haven't any eyes. I mean they just don't seem to be there until a little eye shadow makes them emerge into view.

Maybe it's because of my own particular handicaps, but my advice to all is: when you first become conscious in the morning, get decent. I know some people say have your devotions first, but don't you sort of feel sorry for God when daily he has to face all those millions of hair curlers and old robes? What if *you* were the Almighty, and got prayed to with words spoken through all those unbrushed teeth? It seems to me like the ultimate test of grace.

I look over the day's calendar briefly, next warm up a little and then stair-climb (the world's fastest way to keep in shape, I guess), then shower and put on my face while I'm beginning to talk to God. (I'm just starting to get alert.) Hair next and clothes, and then I'm ready for breakfast, meeting God, and all the day's agenda.

Am I affected by the visual more than most people? Maybe you're like me: you feel better about it all when your person is groomed and your bedroom is groomed, so you do both as quickly as possible. Babies and small children can interrupt, so you don't have a nervous breakdown if you have to go to Plan B, but you know that over the course of your lifetime this is the way it will normally be: first you, then your bed; and then the stage is set to meet God and the beautiful new day.

How little God talks to us in his Word about care of the body! So I don't want to overdo it, either. I suppose all of us women would like to do what Esther did. She got to spend a whole year of her life beautifying herself: six months with creams and oils and then six months with perfumes and cosmetics. Zowee! And this was God's plan for her—to sweep King Ahasuerus off his feet and rescue her people the Jews.

Still, it's certainly God's plan for you and me that we both influence and rescue! How are your elbows, knees, heels? Are you creaming your shoulders, face, chest, arms, and hands, the parts of you that probably get the most sun? How are your hips, thighs, tummy? Do you need to get into that jogging suit and run? How is your hair? Does it have a good cut, and is it clean and healthy? What kind of program are you on to stretch, bend, and stay supple; to stand tall; to be a good advertisement of God's wonderful care of his children?

The first Psalm describes how we should be:

> He will be like a tree firmly planted by streams of water
> [having a hidden source of continual nourishment],
> Which yields its fruit in its season
> [ready constantly to give out to others],
> And its leaf does not wither
> [no sagging, no drying up, ever];
> And in whatever he does, he prospers.

The ninety-second Psalm carries the thought further:

> They will still yield fruit in old age
> [There's no spiritual menopause, friends!];
> They shall be full of sap and very green
> [young-minded, bendable, pliable, vigorous],
> To declare that the Lord is upright.

That's the reason to look good! God's children, when compared with the children of darkness, should declare without a word that God is good. Daniel did it. He and his friends were in a hostile, pagan land. They said, "Look, let us take care of our bodies by our God's standards, and then you judge for yourselves." "And at the end of ten days their appearance seemed better" (Dan. 1:15). Hooray for Jehovah!

Once I was studying Proverbs 31, the description of a "worthy woman," and it struck me in a new light. I noticed that twenty-two verses describe this woman's kindness, godliness, hard work, loving relationships—and only one verse out of the twenty-two describes how she looked. But she looked simply great! Verse twenty-two says, "She makes coverings for herself; her clothing is fine linen and purple." Purple was the fabric of the wealthy.

Seeing this kind of proportion in Proverbs 31—one verse out of twenty-two describes her good looks—I prayed, "Father, I want to give 1/22 of my time to making myself as outwardly beautiful as I can; and I want to give all the rest of my time, 21/22 of my life, to becoming wise, kind, godly, hard-working, and the rest."

I don't mean that this should be a pattern for any other woman; this is simply the pact that I made personally with the Lord. What it means is that out of every twenty-four hours I give a little over one hour to my looks.

Most of that hour is first thing in the morning. I exercise;

I shower; I put on my face, do my hair, and dress. Later in the day I may quickly repair my face and re-dress. At bedtime I exercise again, shower, and slather on body cream. (Before Laney the maid, I allowed only forty-five minutes a day and didn't exercise at night; that left me time to keep the clothes washed, ironed, dry cleaned, and mended. Ray has always polished the shoes on Saturday nights.)

This leaves me just time to get my hair and nails done weekly—and practically no time for shopping. Then that's when God takes over in miracles for me. (Giving God your time is like giving him your money. Give him so much that unless he comes through for you, you can't manage. Then watch your life become a miracle life.)

I'm almost never in stores. A while back I needed two new street-length dresses for church and speaking, and I had about twenty minutes of time.

"Please, Lord, help me," I said, and headed for a Pasadena store that sells purple, if you know what I mean. On the rack inside the door were two dresses, my size, my style, my color, both originally $120 apiece and reduced several times to $45 each! I slipped into them, slipped out, paid my money and left the clerk open-mouthed. And I've felt so comfortable and so right in them ever since!

If I'm out of time and out of money both, someone may give me my need. God will always keep me clothed! And I have the fun of passing on good-looking things to my Christian sisters, too. Love in the Body! It's what life is all about.

But there's another side to this coin. I have promised God to give 1/22 of my time to my looks; if I gave less than that I'd get seedy fast. Before God, as the Old Testament priests sacrificed daily and always kept fire on the altar, I offer him that "one hour plus" of caring for the body. It's for you, Lord.

Concerning that morning ritual: almost all the time goes

for exercising, showering, and doing my face and hair. I need something over five minutes to actually dress. You ask how so fast? *Because I have so few clothes to choose from.*

This is part of my religion! I keep my closet stripped down:

> 4 dressy, street-length outfits
> 4 long casual outfits
> 6 day pants
> 5 day dresses
> 2 sandal dresses
> 3 at-home outfits
> 3 evening and party outfits.

Now, this may be an entirely different kind of wardrobe than you need. Wardrobe should be determined by ministry. Do you know what I mean? Not ministry in the narrow sense of being part of the clergy, but ministry in the broad sense of being put by God into your piece of the world, to live for him and bring your own kind of people around you to know him. I know a beautiful couple at the beach whose only wardrobe is jeans. They love people to Jesus in their jeans and bring them to church in their jeans. Your lifestyle for him will determine your wardrobe.

Then everything in the closet should be ready to grab. Hanging there means it's ready. When something is dirty, it gets washed or cleaned; when it's ripped it gets mended. When something becomes unnecessary or just so-so, give it away.

The world is so needy! All around the globe are women who have so little! And yet they are just as feminine as we are, with the same longings to be pretty. I have bent down and stooped into a thatched hut deep in the jungles of South America and seen a cotton print dress hanging inside, the joy of that little primitive, pudding-bag-shaped woman. Someone she will never see had parted with it, and through missionaries bearing the love of Jesus, it came to her.

Oh, women! It is just wicked to cram and stuff our closets

and drawers with things we seldom wear or don't need to wear! Continually get rid of them! Maybe you'll give your nicest to your best friend; it may look better on her than on you! But keep giving and giving! Keep stripped down! In your wardrobe as well as in the rest of your life, "eliminate and concentrate."

Now, when I buy a dress or a pants outfit or whatever, I don't just buy that alone. I make sure at the time I have everything it needs: shoes, bag, jewelry, underthings, scarf, whatever. I stand before a full-length mirror when it's new and check the whole effect. I jot that complete outfit in my notebook: everything is listed to complete the ensemble. Then it's ready to go. I never have to dawdle over "Does this blouse go with this skirt?" "What beads would look good with this neckline?" I know the whole outfit, and I can fall into it fast and get on to life's more important considerations.

This may sound expensive—but I have one more guiding principle to share. Everyone has a skin color which makes a certain family of colors exactly right for her. Maybe you're a pink, baby blue, lavender, mint green, navy woman. Maybe you're a black, white, red, kelly green, sharp yellow person.

I'm a brown girl: my Bible is brown, my notebook is brown, and all the shoes and handbags I own range from chocolate through the browns to creamy white. Then when I buy a dress (avocado or orange or turquoise or gold or whatever), I probably already have all the accessories I need to go with it. Traveling is easy; I already coordinate. And I can more easily stay stripped down to the minimum.

Here is a little extra hint, a fast and easy one. Every night dump your purse onto your bed. Throw out the gum wrappers, file the receipts or whatever. Then return the minimum contents.

You've noticed my using the words "eliminate and concentrate." I think they're two words that are a key to good living.

You want to manage your time? You eliminate clutter and concentrate on your goals. You want to disciple? You eliminate crowds and concentrate on a few people.

You want to keep a sharp wardrobe, before the Lord Jesus? Eliminate the unnecessary, concentrate on a few "right" outfits in one color scheme.

My goal here is to look really "together," really "kept," in the least possible time; to look "quality" on the least possible money; for 1/22 of my time and concentration to be a woman "clothed in fine linen and purple," and to use 21/22 of my concentration and time to be like this:

> The heart of her husband trusts in her. . . .
> Strength and dignity are her clothing,
> And she smiles at the future.
> She opens her mouth in wisdom,
> And the teaching of kindness is on her tongue.
> She looks well to the ways of her household,
> And does not eat the bread of idleness. . . .
> Charm is deceitful, and beauty is vain,
> But a woman who fears the Lord, she shall be praised.

Sometimes before I speak to groups I pray, "O dear Lord! Cause my heart for you to be twenty-one times more obvious to these women than how I look. Keep the proportions of my life like the woman in Proverbs!"

And I've been praying, "Father, if it's all the same to you, please let this chapter on looks be only 1/22 the length of this book!"

5. Your Goals

"I have a dream," said Martin Luther King. Everyone has to have a dream, to get any place. My dream for right now is to get this book written and blow the mind of every woman living in the Western world. What's yours?

A dream is a precious, exciting thing that carries you forward from day to day; a goal down the way that keeps you on the straight road to get there, looking neither to the right nor to the left; a purpose just for you alone, exhilarating enough to give you momentum for a long time to come.

Every woman has some nebulous thing, enough to make her choose what she chooses. It influences whether she marries or doesn't; gets a job or not; whether she's messy, elegant, too fat, zealously intellectual, sexy, overcautious, organized, deeply spiritual, full of fears—you name it. Something guides us all inside.

Let me put it another way. As I mentioned, last November we were cruising the Mediterranean—160 of us on our hired ship. In the morning all 160 of us would wake up, eat our meals, enjoy each other, go to bed at night, and wake up to another morning. All would seem the same: our shoes were in the same place in the closet; we looked the same to each other. But all was not the same. All 160 of us were in a new place each morning, a different spot in the Mediterranean than we'd ever been before.

So we live our lives. We go through the motions of a day and go to bed at night and wake up to another morning, and we may feel as if we're in the same place. But we're not. We'll never again be where we were yesterday. And we've moved into brand-new, fresh territory.

When we were traveling that Mediterranean, the captain long before had laid out the itinerary. He knew where we were to go each day of the trip, and how to get there. He knew what provisions to take on board before each leg of the journey. He planned ahead, in order not to get caught.

Then, along the way, all kinds of contrary winds and cross currents were trying to take us off-course. The captain had to be continually refocusing, redirecting, recentering us on our destination. Otherwise we wouldn't have ended up in the right place at all.

This is what life-planning is all about. Under that wonderful umbrella of "if God wills," we need to decide where we suspect he'd like us to go. We need to see what provisions are necessary for each leg of the journey, and get them. Then we need to say "no," "no," "no," daily all the rest of our lives to everything that would get us off-course, and keep returning and returning to our personal charts to make sure we're getting there!

Jesus came with the life goal "to seek and to save that which was lost" (Luke 19:10). This gave great pressure and urgency to his decision-making. At one point he even said, "I must journey on today and tomorrow and the next day; for it cannot be that a prophet should perish outside of Jerusalem" (Luke 13:3).

The Apostle Paul knew where he was going; he wrote, "Therefore I run in such a way, as not without aim. . . ." (1 Cor. 9:26). Similarly, Solomon wrote,

Let your eyes look directly ahead,
And let your gaze be fixed straight in front of you.
Watch the path of your feet,
And all your ways will be established.
Do not turn to the right nor to the left;
Turn your foot from evil.

(Prov. 4:25–27)

And again he wrote, "The plans of the diligent lead surely to advantage" (Prov. 21:5).

The first section of my personal notebook is my "goals" section, and I've discovered that my life goals do more than point me in a direction to go; they give me my identity! When you make goals, you discover how you're different from other people; you find out who you are in this world.

I don't open up to you the "goals" section of my notebook easily. When I wrote them—about six years ago—I sincerely thought that they were strictly between God and me, and would always be.

The struggle goes like this: I read that Paul was willing to call himself an open "epistle, . . . read of all men" (2 Cor. 3:2, KJV). I see that he commended the Corinthians for being "followers of the Lord, and of me" (1 Cor. 11:1).

"But, Lord," I say, "I'm no Apostle Paul."

One half of me says that the Word must continually be made flesh—lived out in the lives of people—in order to be authentic.

The other half of me trembles at exposure, at being examined, criticized—and misunderstood.

One half of me says, "Lord, I'm no shining example, but on the other hand, you know I'm no fraud. False modesty would keep me from saying, 'Look, people, following God works!' Fakery would cover your glory at work in one lowly handmaiden. I'm willing to be used, however you want me to be. Be it unto me according to your Word."

The other half of me fears appearing brash, overeager for

the spotlight, obnoxious—posing and bowing when nobody's looking or applauding!

Cover me, O Holy Spirit of God; thine be the Kingdom and the power and the glory.

I was starting to tell you about my goals. At the top of the "life goals" page of my notebook I have written "Iguassu Falls" and "Jeremiah 29:11." They go together in my mind!

Jeremiah 29:11 says, " 'I know the plans that I have for you,' declares the Lord, 'plans for welfare and not for calamity to give you a future and a hope.' "

Iguassu Falls, a series of immense waterfalls bordered by Brazil, Paraguay, and Argentina, is where four of us went last August for "rest and recuperation" after ministering as a team in Bolivia. It is glorious, indescribable. We walked for most of an hour facing almost continuous falls. At the end was the inevitable—a souvenir shop, faced with glass and positioned terribly close to a roaring, majestic cascade. But the clerk sat inside as in a little closed box. The glass wall was so dirty, she could see nothing except the trinkets immediately around her.

"Lord," I prayed, "I don't want to spend my life like that! Clean my windows! Give me a long-range view of your glory!"

"I know the plans that I have for you," he was saying to me, "plans for welfare and not for calamity, to give you a future and a hope."

On my "goals" page, under "Iguassu Falls" and "Jeremiah 29:11," I've written "life purposes" and "life goals." They're what I hope to be, what I hope to do, by the time I die. Most are measurable! Why should we have just vague dreams of turning out to "be a good Christian"? But my "life purposes," my "be" goals, may not be all that measurable:

Inwardly, to see self decrease and God increase, as my un-

pleasant characteristics are crucified and a meek and quiet spirit
becomes an altar of worship to give God pleasure.

Outwardly, to leave a mark on others contemporary to me and
following me, through my life and my talents, which will point
them to God.

You know, the longer I live, the more I realize that all
that's important in this life is God, and people, and connecting the former with the latter. I'm willing to shed a lot of
things to strive after the Important. Aren't you, really?

There's a comforting verse after these purposes jotted down
once as I was praying over them:

> The Lord will accomplish what concerns me;
> Thy loving kindness, O Lord, is everlasting;
> Do not forsake the works of Thy hands.
>
> (Ps. 138:8)

He won't, he won't! You and I are reliant on his mercies.

Following the "life purposes" (what I hope to be), I've
written my "life goals" (what I hope to do). I know the
words don't make that distinction clear, but allow me some
shortcomings. "Give me some slack," as Bud says.

There are six goals, and since I wrote them they haven't
changed, although the first one ought to:

1. To bring glory to God in specific ways of pleasing him
   which I don't yet know how to measure. (Show me,
   help me, Lord.)
2. To bring glory to Ray as his wife, being a credit to him
   and making him proud of me, as well as satisfying him
   personally.
3. To see all four children spiritually settled and fruitful.
   (Three down and one to go on that one. But eleven-
   year-old Nels is coming along.)
4. To write three books, each of which will aid the Body

of Christ and help us retire without penny-pinching. (Oops! Well, you're getting to know the "whole me." This book is number three of that goal.)[1]

5. To write five really successful songs which will greatly bless the church. (I feel I'm only one down and four to go, there. Only "Macedonia" is in world-wide use and in most new hardcover hymnals. There are hundreds more waiting to be discovered!)

6. To serve God together with Ray until we're at least eighty-five—seeing Acts 1:8 fulfilled abundantly.

I hasten to add what follows, Jeremiah 10:23–24:

> I know, O Lord, that a man's way is not in himself;
> Nor is it in a man who walks to direct his steps.
> Correct me, O Lord, but with justice;
> Not with Thy anger, lest Thou bring me to nothing.

I don't deserve a single day, but I must say I want to be like that woman of Proverbs 31:25; she "smiles at the future." "Little old ladies" have been kicked around so long that I'd love to be a way-show-er, an old woman with God's glory on her head who would help change the image.

And I'd love to do it with Ray at my side—an old couple madly in love with the Lord and each other! Why not? I've written beside this, Psalm 61:6: "Thou wilt prolong [my] life; [my] years will be as many generations." But I'm glancing upward: "Only if that's what you had in mind, Lord. . . ."

Acts 1:8, included in that last goal, is a promise God gave Ray years ago—a breathtaking one, to be sure: "You shall receive power when the Holy Spirit has come upon you; and you shall be My witness . . . even to the remotest part of the earth."

---

[1] Number one was *Up with Worship* (Glendale, Cal.: Regal Books, 1975); number two, coauthored with Ray, was *The Best Half of Life* (Glendale, Cal.: Regal Books, 1976).

He was a young blond preacher at the time who hadn't ministered too far away, but whose heart was totally God's, and the Lord has been wonderfully fulfilling that verse in his life ever since. In meditations on this, I have jotted down Psalm 67:1–2:

> God be gracious to us and bless us,
> And cause His face to shine upon us—
> That Thy way may be known on the earth,
> Thy salvation among all nations.

Keep doing it, Lord! To the dirty places, the very hot and cold places, the places of oppression and discouragement, bring Ray—and me, too, when you will—to cause your way to be known!

What are your life dreams and goals? Have you been at conferences and retreats or had other special moments when you dreamed dreams and saw visions? In your highest moments, what has God said to you?

Get away for a day with him. Recapture those visions, or get fresh new ones. Be courageous to make them specific and large—and all for his glory! And

> May He grant you your heart's desires,
> And fulfill all your counsel!
> We will sing for joy over your victory,
> And in the name of our God we will set up our banners.
> May the Lord fulfill all your petitions (Ps. 20:4–5).

Page two of my "goals" section records my current one-year goals. You need to do that, too. If you're young and you figure you've got another fifty years to live, you could fool around for forty-nine years, figuring then you could scramble like mad to get everything done.

But only God knows how long you have, and he isn't going to tell. So this next year is a piece of your life, and if you can see a chunk of your life goals come to pass in this coming year, you could begin to say, "Hey, I think I'm going to make it! I think I'm going to be one of the winners!" As Ray says,

It's hard
By the yard,
But a cinch
By the inch!

The psalmist says it better: "So teach us to number our days, that we may present to Thee a heart of wisdom" (Ps. 90:12).

My aims this year come out of my life goals, of course, but they're divided into the three priorities.[2] I see now what I didn't see when I wrote life goals six years ago, that grouping goals under the three priorities helps me become a balanced, whole person—reaching in correct proportions upward to God and outward to my fellow Christians and to the needy world.

First, I've written Psalms 23:3 and 25:12 from *The Living Bible;* they're great eliminate-and-concentrate verses! "He helps me do what honors him the most." And, "Where is the man who fears the Lord? God will teach him how to choose the best."

Under Priority One:
1. To use ACTS every quiet time. (That's a helpful formula for prayer: Adoration, Confession, Thanksgiving, and Supplication. I desperately need more ACT and less S-S-S-!)
2. To become a woman of prayer, moment by moment; not "stewing" but praying; turning every situation into an opportunity for talking continually with God. (This is a very measurable goal for me. I can make eloquent speeches straightening out my husband, the Board of Trustees, etc.—speeches nobody ever hears, rehearsed

---

[2] See chapter 2, "Reshaping Your Life to Three Priorities."

when I'm ironing, or when I ought to be sleeping. I can sound so convincing, and every word hits its mark, and when I'm done I'm nothing but frustrated! "Not stewing but praying" is a slogan in my heart this year, to "cast my burdens on the Lord.")

3. To read the *New American Standard Bible* through. (I'm on target: Proverbs finished today, July 5.)
4. To increase my prayer life by:
   a. Praying over goals three times weekly;
   b. Praying over members of each small group [3] three times weekly. (The first year I made one-year goals I found not many got realized. Then it dawned on me that there's nothing magic about writing goals down on a piece of paper! It was only as I brought them back to God over and over that they began to be the true basis of my living and planning and doing.)

Under Priority Two:

1. To support and satisfy Ray in every way possible. (A good marriage, even when you're as much in love as we are, is an unrelenting discipline, to be shored up by constant prayer.)
2. To have prayer and Bible study daily with Nels (I'm not doing too well here. I notice the recent dates on our times together: June 8, 13, 14, 17, 18, 21, 24, 27, July 3 . . . Lord, help me!)
3. To function as a loving, praying sister in Christ to Beulah, Betty, Doris, Peg, Fran, Joan—others, too—the members of my current small groups.

Under Priority Three:

1. (This one's exciting, and every woman should have something similar.) To lead 6 people to know Christ; to lead 4 to be committed to morning and evening church; to lead 4 to be committed to adult Sunday School; to lead 4 to be committed to small groups; to lead 4 into

---

[3] See chapter 9, "Your Closest Relationships."

church membership. (After all, I'm only doing people a favor! And if I say I long to make a mark on people for God, why shouldn't these marks be specific and measurable?)

2. To finish well two books: *The Best Half of Life* (done) and———(whatever the title of this will be; the baby doesn't have a name yet).

Well, your goals will be very different from mine—but wonderful! God makes no two flowers or snowflakes or women alike.

But then, you probably need to break down your year goals into something smaller: a quarter? a month? or just a week? When Ray and I go away for our monthly "think days," we evaluate how our year's goals are going and consider what should happen in the next month. Some people I know make out a specific calendar a week at a time, with weekly goals listed. I fear getting to be a "paper person," who is so busy planning there's not much time to realize the plans. Yet, if at any stage of life you feel you're "flying by the seat of your pants," taking each day as it comes without having anticipated it, planned for it, shaped it, and prayed over it, then take time off and get back to poring over your goals. Then you will control your days, instead of letting them control you.

We'll talk about the daily process in the next chapter. It's wonderful, though, how living by goals makes each day—indeed, each hour!—so precious and important. And daily duties get eliminated, streamlined, or become very important in the light of your whole life! Praise God, what fun!

Alexander Whyte, the day before he died, wrote these words: "A life spent in the service of God and communion with Him is the most comfortable and pleasant life that anyone can live in this world." [4]

---

[4] Quoted by William Paul in Keswick "Daily Readings" calendar, 21 February 1976.

6. *Your Daily Scheduling*

Our friend Jack La Lanne came bouncing onto the television screen one morning, muscles rippling as usual, and said, pointing his finger at me, "You have twenty-four hours every day to do whatever you want. And you are the sum total of how you use those hours."

I told him, "I know it's true, Jack. You yourself are the visible proof of what you've been doing with your time, and I want to be proof of mine."

Dear fellow-human in this world, our minutes and hours and days are so precious! But they will be largely wasted unless they flow out of predetermined goals and strategies.

"Most people don't think in terms of minutes," says Alan Lakein, president of the only company in America devoted exclusively to time-management. "They waste all the minutes. Nor do they think in terms of their whole life. They operate in the mid-range of hours or days. So they start over again every week, and spend another chunk unrelated to their lifetime goals. They are doing a random walk through life, moving without getting anywhere." [1]

---

[1] Jane O'Reilly, "How to Get Control of Your Time (and Your Life)," *New York Magazine*, 17 January 1972.

The Los Angeles Herald Examiner had an interesting article recently entitled "Timely Tips for Managing Your Minutes."[2] Most of it was made up of interviews with famous people on how they manage their time.

Executive Fred Harris lives a ten-minute walk from his work in downtown New York. (When Ray's secretary Lorrayne shifted from World Vision to Lake Avenue Congregational Church, she moved from her apartment five minutes from World Vision to an apartment five minutes from the church, although the two are only 30 minutes apart. Some women would have been tempted not to go through the hassle of moving, but in the succeeding years Lorrayne has saved at least sixty minutes every day.)

Christine Beshar and her husband are both lawyers, and they know how to delegate responsibility. Their seventeen-year-old daughter has her own checking account and does most of the food shopping, and two nights a week the children cook dinner.

Laurie Woodruff stacks simultaneous activities: he reads a novel and dries his hair while eating his lunch. (I do the same; for instance, I don't shave my legs, I cream the hair off so I can be studying at the same time.) Barbara Walters echoes, "Like most busy people I do three things at once." Then she adds this cute sentence: "Women must balance their time more than men because they don't have wives."

The point of all this is not to feel driven—although people not under God's authority may well feel that way! The point is to get done as efficiently as possible the necessary mechanics of life, so that you can give yourself to what you really want to do—like getting to know God better, and fulfilling your gifts, and bringing others to know him.

So how are you going to control your time? It probably won't be hard for you to sit down and make a list of bad habits and obvious time leaks.

---

[2] Ron Scherer, 14 December 1975.

There is also the trick of never handling a piece of paper twice. Paper shuffling can be a great waster of time! Read your mail with a red pencil; then you'll only reread key items when you answer it. Or act on it immediately and throw it away.

Read a newspaper as you would a page of a history book: read what will be important to the unfolding of world or local history, and skip all the rest.

And keep up to date two things: a calendar and a notebook. The calendar stays at your desk. The notebook is small enough to go with you wherever you go. The calendar is beside the telephone, and appointments get written into it as soon as you make them.

Then the appointments get transferred to your notebook, and if you turn out to be like me, you'll live out of your notebook![3] The first section of my notebook is calendar pages, a page for every day. Here I plot my life: my appointments, the working out of my goals, times for rest, and times proportioned to be with people I love, so that none are missed over a span of time.

The "to do" aspect of my notebook calendar pages is crucial. In the "B.N." years ("Before Notebook"), I wrote lists on scraps of paper—"to do" lists, shopping lists. And then, where did I put that scrap? Or I thought of something I had to do next week, next month, and I just thought, "I'll try to remember."

But now my notebook never leaves me. (I hear former Congresswoman Shirley Chisholm carries a pocket calendar and does the same thing.) Anywhere I am and I think, "Oh, I mustn't forget to do so-and-so," I not only write it in my notebook, but I write it on the day when it should be done. Then it's out of my head and into my notebook. This includes shopping items, things I need to tell people—every reminder I need for living.

[3] See chapter 9.

I keep about three months' worth of pages ahead in my notebook. I put an arrow by the most important items, to give them first attention. I cross them off as I do them. At the end of a day I rewrite on a future day any that didn't get done—and I throw the old day's page away.

The calendar pages get filled with everything from the crazy to the humdrum to the exotic. Look for a vacuum cleaner. Twice a month, deposit paycheck, write and mail bills. Remind Nels to clean the hamster's cage. 7:30 P.M.: deacons here for dessert. 11:30 A.M.: Fly Northwest Orient to Honolulu. Pray over possible disciples for fall. Three nights in a row, warm oil in my ears! For six weeks the top of every day said "George"; at one of our couples' meetings I'd promised to pray for George every day until a certain deadline.

Last winter sometime, I was driving along in Pasadena and I suddenly thought, "When was the house last checked for termites?" At the stop light I pulled my notebook to me on the car seat and wrote "Termites?" on April 16. (Naturally you can't fork out an unknown sum until after income tax time.) So when April 16 finally came, there was my reminder. The termite people said it had been five years, and yes, we needed a little work.

Beautiful system! Let me list several benefits. First, the pressures are off me to remember things. (Ray says I'm more organized now. I'm really not; my *notebook* is organized, and I do whatever it tells me to.)

Second, my weeks and months are evenly scheduled. My notebook regulates the flow! For instance, I've written in on a day early in November to order Christmas cards. I mark out a few days after Thanksgiving to address the envelopes. Last year when a possible appointment loomed for the first week in December, I'd already written that it was the best time for Christmas shopping, so I didn't take the appointment. I can predict my pace and therefore regulate my pace.

Third, I can see at a glance whether my life is *important*

enough! If I make a notebook of my days and the pages are too empty or the lists filled with trivia, I can quickly see that I'm not being a good steward of God's precious time. Or that I'm not using my gifts, although this is seldom my particular problem.

(Do I come across too smug and sure of myself? You don't know how I can agonize behind the scenes. For instance, I just left this manuscript for a couple of days and then came back to it, approaching it with this lovely, pink-edged image of it in my mind as a spiritual book to draw women everywhere to God; and the first thing I read when I picked it up was "I don't shave my legs, I cream the hair off. . . ."

"Dear God," I gasped, "I must be out of my mind! If you don't help me, this thing will be nothing but repulsive trivia, and I'll be the laughingstock of everyone."

So please be kind enough to sympathize a little with my "backside" feelings.)

Fourth—and this definitely was my problem—my notebook keeps me from time-wasting and the resultant uneven bunching. I don't dare let the days "come as they will." First I'd procrastinate; then I'd be pressured by deadlines.

And fifth, my notebook forces me to put first things first. Oh, dear, important woman in this world, life is so precious and so brief! Perhaps by the time you read this, I'll be gone. That's why God is urging me along to get this book written, so that hundreds of thousands, perhaps millions, of women will get some "handles" on life, to grab hold of quickly and get reshaped, reoriented to life's highest and best. While there's time!

Your life didn't start too well? Let it finish well! That's far better than the reverse.

Eric Hoffer said this wonderful thing:

> The genuine creator creates something that has a life of its own, something that can exist and function without him. This

is true not only of the writer, artist, and scientist, but of creators in other fields.

A creative organizer creates an organization that can function well without him. When a genuine leader has done his work his followers will say, "we have done it ourselves," and feel that they can do great things without a great leader.

With the noncreative it is the other way around: in whatever they do, they arrange things so that they themselves become indispensable.[4]

I say this honestly: God can take me any time. But I pray this book will become a true friend of yours, to steer you and guide you to God, to an integrated life, and to putting first things first.

Start now. Here is a list of things you can do when you're tempted to dawdle—or watch TV indiscriminately:

1. Exercise
2. Memorize Scripture
3. Look over your coming calendar, and prepare what to wear
4. Give yourself a pedicure
5. Write a list of your blessings
6. Walk around your house critically: adjust, rearrange, throw out, give away
7. Cook ahead for the freezer
8. Cream yourself all over
9. Read part of an important book
10. Clean out your cosmetics drawer
11. Write a letter to an old friend
12. Do your nails
13. Weed your garden

---

[4] *Reader's Digest,* August 1971, Eric Hoffer is a San Francisco longshoreman and philosopher whose books include *The True Believer* and *First Things, Last Things.*

14. Bring your recipe file up to date
15. Encourage a Christian friend by telephone, someone you don't usually call
16. Put all those old photos into albums
17. Take a walk in the park
18. Nap on a slant board, or with your feet up
19. Have a prolonged time talking with God: partly on your knees, partly standing with hands raised, partly on your face before him on the floor
20. Polish the silver
21. Write a poem (don't be silly; everybody does)
22. Write your pastor an encouraging note.

7. Your Growing Life

I'm sitting beside the yacht basin in Honolulu harbor, and stretched out in front of me are hundreds of yachts bobbing in their slips.

I'm looking at sleek white cabins and fun-colored sails. But when one of these boats puts out to sea, everybody aboard had better be thankful for what I can't see, as well—the keel. Without a good-sized keel the boat would quickly capsize and everybody would be gulping sea water.

The importance of the invisible! This is true of any life as well. If all of our life is visible to others, from the time we get up in the morning until we fall into bed at night, then we'll be as unsteady as a ship with no keel. Indeed, the more of us is invisible, hidden from the world in quiet, in study, in planning, and in prayer, the more effective our visible life will be.

Everybody knows stories of someone who says, "If I have a normal day, I can get by with one hour of planning and quiet with God. But if I have a very busy day, I need at least two or more."

I have to get away from the house for these quiet times. Of

course for years I couldn't, when the big children were little. But I could have, sooner than I thought of it; as soon as little Buddy was in kindergarten, I could have slipped away from the house.

In the house I see too much to do! Don't you? I'm having a great time in the Book of Jeremiah and suddenly I think, "Did I take the synthetics out of the dryer?" Or the phone rings. Or somebody's at the door.

When Nels is breakfasted and put off to school, then I go to a quiet corner of a restaurant where I know no one, and there I have breakfast, plan, read, and pray (I write out my prayers).

Or in pretty weather I just park the car somewhere where I'm anonymous, and sit in the car.

Or I go to a secluded couch in the nook of a hotel.

For everyone, God will give a spot. But if you're stuck at home for now, vow not to answer the phone or the doorbell. Turn your chair to the corner of the room if you must. Shut out the world! Jesus called it "entering into your closet" (Matt. 6:6). For you, that may be the bathroom. But the quality of your life will be determined by the amount of time you spend alone with God in reading, praying, and planning.

What makes a wedding an exquisite occasion? Every detail has been thought out and planned, maybe for months. What makes an exquisite life? Everything is thought out and prayed over, behind the scenes, well in advance. Then you're truly ready to live—ready with what to wear, where to go, what to do, what to say, whom to be with, and so on.

Ray's morning quiet time includes praying over his schedule for that day. With date book in hand, he prays over each of his appointments; he prays for the interruptions, the unexpected telephone calls, any unpleasant surprises. As the day goes along he's not easily ruffled, because he says he's already "got it covered." So it is with the godly man in Psalm 112:7: "He will not fear evil tidings; his heart is steadfast, trusting in the Lord." A mother of small children gets a dozen unpleasant surprises a day! She needs time to settle her heart with God and be a growing Christian.

The keel determines the stability of a ship. Our invisible times of quiet determine the stability of our lives.

What are your papers, your magazines, your books? They tell volumes about whether you're a dawdler, like a sheep nibbling on any tuft of grass that comes along, or whether you're going after what's important to you. They represent a quiet part of your life—part of your ship's keel. They should be a reflection of the depths of you.

You have a special interest; what is it? Housekeeping? Ham radio? Dog training? High-diving? Collect books on whatever turns you on; subscribe to a magazine on the subject; find a pen pal with the same interest; clip and file articles. Get to really know what you know!

Eliminate and concentrate! Throw the rest of the clutter away; better yet, recycle the paper stuff and give the old unread books to a library or the Salvation Army. But begin to build a personal library which is truly meaningful to you.

My friend Ginny's first husband was a lawyer whose off-duty interest was the exploration of space. By the time he died, he had collected so many books on the subject that California Institute of Technology, their recipient, called them the world's finest library on the subject and built a building just to house them!

You probably won't do that, but your collection of whatever it is will be a meaningful contribution to somebody someday. Furthermore, it may become a new career for you, a way to earn money after the children are grown, or a job you'll switch to after this one. Who knows?

Most important, every Christian needs to become a specialist in God! Many of your magazines, books, and papers need to feed your spirit. These lives of ours are to get us ready for eternity, you know! So we must "be diligent [or study, as the King James Version says] to present [ourselves] approved to God as [workmen] who [do] not need to be ashamed, handling accurately the word of truth" (2 Tim. 2:15). We need to be knowledgeable women—knowledgeable in doctrine and in Christian world affairs. This world globe has a timetable with it; we need to be alert, discerning the times and living with care.

Submerge as much of your day as you can, to make it your invisible keel, by eliminating less important things. You need time to look into the face of God, time to read and study his Word systematically, time to think and plan for your life, time to praise, time to intercede, time to get wisdom for handling people and for making decisions.

If you're in the years of early housekeeping and small children, you need time for what Pat King calls "backward planning" for each day, time to sit at your kitchen table early in the day and work out the day backwards:

> Let's say the goal this particular Monday morning is order by noon. . . .
> "The kitchen is the biggest mess of all—it should take an hour. So . . . I must start the kitchen at eleven. The bathroom will take 20 minutes, so I should start it at 10:40. It's going to take fifteen minutes to put away everything in the front room. . . ." [1]

So she hustles through the morning with one eye on the clock, and disciplines herself to stay on schedule. It must work; she has ten children and looks beautiful! And it's true that if you don't have that period of time to think it all through first, you'll forget things, duplicate, backtrack, and spin your wheels.

If you're working outside the home, there is much to pray over and plan for, to balance job and home management

---

[1] Pat King, *How Do You Find the Time?* (Edmonds, Wash.: Aglow Publications, 1975), p. 79.

and make the precious hours count. And the most healing, productive task you have is just to sit before God, adoring him, communicating with him, enjoying him. That you can't rush!

Part of my personal notebook is for Bible study. Recently, watching a televised Billy Graham Crusade in Lubbock, Texas, I heard the remarkable testimony of the quarterback of the University of Oklahoma's football team. Out of his mouth poured beautiful Scriptures. Then he said it had been his habit since junior high school to study his Bible each day with notebook and pencil in hand. No wonder his mouth and his heart are full of God's truth!

I don't know where I've been all my life, but I didn't start systematically writing during my Bible readings until recently. For preparing to teach Bible classes, yes. But that was for someone else's heart, not mine!

And I must say that over the years I must have forgotten most of the wonderful truths that grabbed me at the moment, because I didn't write them down.

There's value in marking our Bibles, of course; daily I jot down thoughts and cross references in the margins. But I didn't realize, when I started making systematic notes, all the rich material I'd be adding to my store, ready to give out!

If you say you don't know how to study the Bible, don't worry. Just start in! That's why God has given his Holy Spirit to you, to teach you. Amazing what 1 John 2:27 says: "You have no need for any one to teach you; but . . . His anointing teaches you about all things."

Ray's first love and greatest gift, I guess, is preaching God's Word. It's certainly his passion to study the Scriptures correctly and feed his flock a balanced diet of truth. But in all his years he's never sat under expository Bible preaching; seminary helped in many practical ways, but not in learning the Bible; and he's never been to a Bible school.

So where did he learn all he knows—everything which for seventeen years has been broadcast weekly halfway around the world, and taught millions? He's learned it just the way you and I can—from digging on his own. From asking good teachers for suggestions on study books. From reading the book itself, and its marginal notes and cross references. From tracking down word studies in concordances. From praying over it. I know this, because for many years he has let me get out of town with him one day a week and study with him. What a privilege!

And you know what? Whether you're a long-time Bible student or a novice, the Holy Spirit is your personal teacher, and he will grade the material for you! Each time you read it, he'll make it right just for your level of understanding at that time. He's wonderful!

So set aside time each day; have your notebook and pencil ready. Begin with one book or one section, probably something in the New Testament if it's new to you. Note the key thoughts, key words; how the passage fits what's before and after; what you don't understand, to ask somebody; how it can help your life that very day. Dig in!

For the last five years I've read the Bible through each year. (More than once I've sat in our church watch night service on December 31, sneaking in the last few pages of Revelation to get under the wire.) This is quick reading: five pages a day will do it.

You see, there are many ways to study. To study, for instance, a mountain, you can get down on your hands and knees with a magnifying glass and see what kind of worms and bugs it has, whether the soil is sandy or rocky, what kind of plants grow on it. Or you can go up in a helicopter and study the mountain's topography—where its watershed is, its timberline, and so on.

Study your Bible both ways! Sometimes on your hands and knees, examining one verse or one word in detail. Sometimes sweeping through it to see the peaks and valleys. You'll see entirely different things, each way.

What do you do with all this accumulating material? Have a simple file system with a folder marked for each book from Genesis to Revelation. When you finish studying a book or section, drop your notes into the right folder. Gradually you'll acquire a great deal of material, amassed by you personally, on the Book which God wants you to know better than any other. You'll be more and more ready to pass it on to others, which is what he's put you on earth to do. You'll begin to be engrossed in that which is the truly and eternally Important!

Betty is my neighbor across the street. She and Dick both accepted Christ year before last, and they've been two of the fastest growing "spiritual babies" Ray and I have ever had. Recently I discovered why.

Lately Betty's been redoing their large, gracious home, one of Pasadena's loveliest, and she invited me upstairs to see what the decorator had done with her private room for special interests. One section compartmentalized her sewing; another organized her entertaining notebooks, her recipes and menus, her guest lists. . . . And here was her Bible study file. Everything I've taught Betty every Wednesday morning for almost two years, all the notes she'd taken, were filed away in beautiful order, ready to be restudied or to be passed along.

No wonder, then, that recently when Kay, next-door to me, expressed an interest in studying the Bible, Betty was ready to take on her own first disciple, every Friday morning. Kay, the new spiritual baby, is thrilled; Betty, the parent, is thrilled; and I, the spiritual grandparent, am delirious with joy.

Betty's diligent life behind the scenes, the keel of her ship, has made her steady and knowledgeable. This is how 2 Timothy 2:1–2 works out in any woman's life: "Be strong in the grace that is in Christ Jesus, and the things which you have heard from me. . . . these entrust to faithful [people], who will be able to teach others also."

8.   *Your Life Behind the Scenes*

Where is the real you? It's deep inside of you, where your thinking and deciding really take place. Your life, as Ray says, is like a wheel, with the hub the true center of who you really are. The rim is all the places where your life touches this world, where there's apt to be plenty of friction, heat and dust.

But in the center is the true you. If you have made God your highest priority of all, he is there. You are learning to abide in him, and he in you. There is calm, there is peace. He is your refuge, to which you continually run. He is organization, and living in him you sense control and plan. He is spirit—your living and breathing, your laughter and tears—and all of it becomes holy because his spirit is holy. Wonderful! Alleluia!

If this is true, your mental and emotional life should reflect his presence, whether there's nobody around but you, or kids everywhere: "Whatever is true, . . . honorable, . . . right, . . . pure, . . . lovely, . . . of good repute [or attractive], . . . let your mind dwell on these things" (Phil. 4:8). (Yes, God says this even to mothers, and he never asks anything of you that he doesn't also give all the ability necessary to carry out.)

And also, if this is true (that God is at your life's center) then your immediate surroundings ought also to reflect him. Your immediate surroundings—your drawers and closets, your bedside table, your desk—are the filmiest clothing of your most personal, private life. Even if you have ten children, those areas should be yours alone, and they should reflect the order and peace of your inner life with God.

The smaller your family, the more the circumference of your immediate surroundings expands. If you're the unmarried president of a bank, you may have a whole penthouse to yourself. If you have many children, you may not have much of the house to call your own. If you share a college dorm room with two other girls, you have one third of a room. Whatever is yours, let it reflect the beauty of a woman whose heart is with God.

If you say you don't have enough drawers and closet space for everything, you own too many things. Give away, pare down, and let your intimate rooms and drawers and closets look serene and controlled—*kept,* like you.

I must say that all through the years, my chief delight has not been to wax or scrub. Raising four children didn't make house cleaning any easier, either. But I've always figured if I could make a room look *pretty,* pride would force me to keep it passably vacuumed and dusted! What has disciplined me is the philosophy that you can't see a daisy in a bud vase if there's a sock in the middle of the floor.

So even when Ray was a student at Princeton Seminary and we were in a tiny student apartment with three babies, the children's play area was either a gated-off space with all their toys, or out-of-doors. Some parts of the little apartment were for adults only.

And the picking up goes on forever, doesn't it! Dirty clothes must go into the hamper just as fast as dirty thoughts in our minds must be done away with. Both are unworthy of lying around, untended to, in the life of a child of God!

What's on your bedside table? Maybe a lamp, an intimate picture or two framed with love, and if you live in a kind climate or can afford it, one flower. Sort out everything else— throw it away, give it away, put it away. Have you a drawer in your bedside table? Put in your bedtime reading materials. No drawer? Put them in a pretty basket under your table. A few areas like this are sacrosanct, off-limits to the children.

My most luxurious feeling comes from seeing a fresh flower in a bud vase where I brush my teeth; it makes me happier there than in the living room! It gives me the feeling of truly "living from the inside out," of having my most intimate life with God beautiful and orderly, whether the outer circumference always is or not. If I'm living with him there, I'm in the eye of the storm, and the outer areas of life can't touch the real me.

Next closest to God in my life is my husband. For you it may be a husband or, because of sheer proximity, a roommate. Honor that person by looking nice as much as you can. This life isn't really "behind the scenes"; this is "living from the inside out." Instead of being a fake with a mask on, your public life will reflect your private life. And your private life will have beauty and order. Why are so many people polite to strangers, and shrews with those closest to them? The closer people get to you, if you're "abiding in God," the more enjoyable you should be. Your husband or roommate isn't really blessed by your belching, picking your toes, throwing your dirty underwear around. . . . Read Song of Solomon again to soak up the atmosphere of God's idea of a beautiful woman: her perfume, her washed feet, her total femininity.

One time Ray got to pay a visit to some of the world's leading race horses, worth hundreds of thousands of dollars. Their stalls were completely padded, to guard against any infection from little scratches and bumps.

How much more should God's woman, so needed in this world and precious to God, guard her inner chambers! Don't let cheap music blare or vulgar television shows ruin the atmosphere. Don't yell at the kids. When you can help it, don't bruise or become bruised by those close-in people around you.

You say, "But when do I get to be the real me? When do I get to express myself?" This is the very thing I'm talking about!

A generation ago, worldliness was smoking, dancing, drinking, lipstick, and playing cards. Today, worldliness is substituting for Christianity a pseudo-psychological, me-pampering, feelings-oriented religion that says, "If it feels good, do it." Many Christians haven't read enough Scripture to catch the real possibility of holy living. The "real you" that I'm talking about should be "in God," practicing his presence, living in holiness. Of course you should express yourself! When Jesus is the control-center of your heart and life, you'll express yourself in blessing, not cursing—and it will be the "real you." You won't be bottled-up and inhibited, trying to hold in that temper and keep shut the lid to Pandora's box. You will truly put away "all bitterness and wrath and anger and clamor and slander, . . . along with all malice." And you'll "be kind to one another, tender-hearted, forgiving each other, just as God in Christ also has forgiven you" (Eph. 4:31–32)! Once in a while you'll include a loving rebuke just as you expect to be lovingly rebuked in return (Gal. 6:1–2).

Beauty in relationships, beauty in physical surroundings, in your private life! Amen, Lord! So be it! And when cursing instead of blessing slips out of your mouth, James 3 says that's not the normal; that's the abnormal, the unhealthy. Say you're sorry right away, to God and your loved one, and get back again to the health and fun and beauty of blessing each other.

Relationships within the private life are forever shifting and changing. They need constant vigilance in prayer and a thousand, thousand hugs, kisses, pats, *"I love you*'s" and

"*I'm sorry*'s." If you live alone and don't get in on this kind of stretching and growth, get all the deeper inside part of the total Christian family—the Body of Christ—to expose yourself to all this. It will keep you from isolation, which is deadly.

Now back to physical surroundings. Bathroom counters (like kitchen counters) can be disaster areas. Keep yours almost totally bare; if you haven't space in cupboards or drawers for your make-up, put it all in a pretty basket. You'll clean the counter oftener if you only have a basket to pick up! But if your cosmetics are in drawers, it may be time for reorganization: hair items here, face needs here, body creams here. The items you haven't used for a while, give away or throw away. Do the same to the medicine chest.

Now for your clothes. Maybe you want to go all the way and repaper your closet, paint matching shelves, border the shoe boxes with paper and ribbon; you know how far you have a desire to go—or dare to, if you share it with someone!

But everything in your closets and dressers needs reexamination. If you haven't worn it in a year, why haven't you? Because you've gained or lost weight? That's another whole area you need to lay out before the Lord, and probably before a doctor, submit to what you're told to do, and get yourself to the proper weight. There are so many books on the subject of weight-control, I won't add words to this one to discuss it. Certainly it's a key factor in being a beautiful woman for God. And I'm just as serious about the worrier who's too thin because of a tied-up stomach!

Both problems are not too big for God. He wants you to be one of the winners, and he can help you get to and keep the weight that is right for you. Then all the clothes you have will be one size, the right size, and all else should be given away.

Before you ever check out your present clothes, sit down in front of a large mirror with plenty of good daylight and hold colors under your face. What makes you look especially pretty? If the autumn colors do it, you're a brown gal like me, and you've found the key to your wardrobe. If black and white make you dazzle, they're your foundation. If the pastels are your cup of tea, navy could be your basic accessory color.

By the color test, you may see clothing right now in your closet you need to give away—or eventually. I know it takes time and money to change over to a coordinated wardrobe.

Once past the color test, next try on every one of your pieces of clothing, with shoes, bag, and jewelry, in front of a full-length mirror. First question: does the clothing call attention to itself, or does it make a great background for you? You have the choice of being thought of as a clotheshorse, or as a beautiful woman! Then, how are the seams, the zipper, the buttons, the hemlines? Notice the bust darts, the fit of the shoulders.

How about the total fit, the necklines. Are they modest? You don't want to be just a classy woman; you want to be *God's* classy woman. Look critically.

Does the outfit do the most for you? If you're hippy you don't need a gathered skirt or huge hip pockets. Unless you're willowy-slender, watch the layers.

The shoes should usually match or be darker than the skirt; if the skirt is a print, they should match the darkest color. Do the shoes and bag have the right "feel" for the clothes? Spectators demand a sporty outfit. A silky dress may need patent pumps. Is the need for chunky jewelry, dainty jewelry, or maybe, refreshingly, none at all? Check the total look, the focal points; "eliminate and concentrate!"

Check your underwear. Do you have the right underpinnings for each outfit? Then throw away what's lived its total life. Check your panty hose, and put the ones with runs in a separate box to go with pants.

Make a list of each complete outfit, and give away everything else you don't need. Somebody else does!

Probably your drawers need organizers. Your closet needs a

place for belts, for bags, for shoes, for hats. Have you a spare closet or a container for out-of-season clothes? Also, keep an evening outfit, a play outfit, or whatever ready for a sudden occasion.

Are you using all your closet space? How about storage boxes on the top shelf, more rods and hooks? You ought to buy shoe trees. And if you can afford it, buy padded hangers and give all those wire ones back to the cleaners.

Are your dresser, your closet, your armoire or whatever—all your dressing needs—close together so you can dress in one spot with everything within reach? Maybe the bedroom needs rearranging.

(Important note: if you live with a husband, be sure his conveniences are met first, that he has the largest closet, the most convenient space. All through the years this silently testifies that you care for him, that you're concerned about his needs first.)

Now, step back and look. Is there a full-length mirror? Is there a place for everything, and everything in its place?

Now wander through the rest of your apartment or home. You're moving out from the center, and after the center is right, the rest is an extension of that. By "right" I don't mean expensive, but I mean two things: organized and pretty.

Is there simply too much of everything? Too much furniture, too many things? Give away, throw away, and call the Salvation Army.

Are the colors right? You may like coordinated flow, or you may like planned potpourri. But if you need to paint or slip-cover, do it.

What needs organizing? Alphabetize your addresses or recipes or whatever. Group your games. File your old photos. Systematize your sewing equipment. What haven't you touched or used in six months ɔr a year? Unless they're books or treasures, give them away.

What needs hiding? When you clear all the unused stuff

out of your kitchen cupboards you'll have room to put in the toaster, the mixer, the coffee pot. You still haven't room? Then clothe them in matching jackets. Maybe your sewing area needs a pretty screen in front of it.

See if your kitchen counters can be almost bare; then add one thing just because it looks good: a bowl of fruit, a happy plant, glass canisters of raw things.

To give your home or apartment at least an illusion of beauty, let the most obvious eye-catchers in each room be beautiful, not utilitarian.

You see not the ironing board, but a rose.

Right?

9. *Your Closest Relationships*

I let you see my "life purposes" in chapter five. The second one was "Outwardly, to leave a mark on others contemporary to me and following me, through my life and my talents, which will point them to God."

"To leave a mark on others"! A Hollywood partygoer I read about doesn't expect to. She says, "The whole idea of life is living with enjoyment, as much enjoyment as you can from a very imperfect world. If you fail to look at your life that way, you can go right through it with absolutely a zero at the end—I mean, when you disappear, so what? You haven't left a footprint, a mark, or anything at all."

Poor, poor dear! Dressed to the teeth, coifed and jeweled, all dressed up for life, and nowhere to go! Contrast that with fitting your life into God's plans for you. Then only he himself knows how deep, how wide will be your mark on eternity!

One day a fellow approached Jesus, scuffed his toe in the dirt, couldn't think of a great conversation-opener and so he said, "Sir, where are you staying around here?" Jesus spent hours with him and revealed to him the fact that he was the long-awaited Messiah (John 1:35–41).

The fellow turned out to be Andrew, who went and got his brother Simon and introduced him to Jesus.

The result for Andrew and Simon? Seeing thousands converted in one day, writing letters which became part of God's sacred Word, and becoming two of the foundation stones of the eternal Church (Eph. 2:20)—not to mention having their names written upon the final Heavenly City of God (Rev. 21:14).

How's that for making a mark, when all you did was approach Jesus and ask an ordinary question?

When you link up with him, you have gotten to where the action is, and only God himself will determine what the eternal effects will be.

And he commands us to be diligent and deliberate about making our lasting marks on others. That's our script in his play. He spells it out in Matthew 28:18–20: "All authority has been given to me. . . . Go therefore and make disciples of all the nations, . . . teaching them to observe all that I commanded you; and lo, I am with you always."

"Make disciples"? Jesus said this to his own disciples, so naturally they knew what he meant. "I've been with you at close range for three years. I chose you out of the multitudes and have poured my truth into you. Now I'm leaving, so you turn around and each choose a few, and teach them everything I've taught you."

Soon came Pentecost! Pow! Explosion! Fireworks! 120 believers had 3,000 new converts to assimilate. How would they do it? No problem, with Jesus' last words ringing in their ears. Each veteran took on an average of 25 spiritual babies, absorbing them into his life at close range. He taught them everything he'd learned from Jesus ("the apostles' teaching," Acts 2:42); they fellowshiped; they ate meals together; he took them along to worship services.[1]

Where did all this take place? In two locations: in the temple, where there would be room for all, and in homes,

---

[1] "Prayer," in Acts 2:42, is actually in the Greek "the prayers," identical to Acts 3:1, "the prayers" conducted at stated hours in the temple.

where obviously they met in small groups (Acts 2:46). How often? Daily. And this new Body lifestyle, sketched out for us in Acts 2, was so successful that soon the 3,000 grew to 5,000 (Acts 4:4).

Discipling is what we're for, in this world! We're not for adoration and worship of God only, although that's number one. If that were all we're for, God could take us straight to heaven, where our worship would be undistracted.

No, the reason he leaves us here a while is so that we can make a mark on others before we go. We lived for several months in a country which punishes its citizens with death if they become Christians. One night we were taken secretly to have a private dinner with a young man of that land who loves Jesus with all his heart.

How handsome he was, and what an attractive personality he had! He sat on the floor across from us and said, "I can never have a girl friend. I don't even think about a wife. I know before too long they'll get me.

"But, oh," he said, and leaned across so earnestly, "my burning desire is to replace myself with several other Christians before I go!"

The Hollywood partygoer didn't know what life is all about, but that young fellow did.

Recently I read this comment on 1 Corinthians 15:58, "Be steadfast, . . . knowing that your labor is not in vain in the Lord":

A solid bar, five inches thick, actually bent under the pressure of my hand! I couldn't have believed it, but a remarkable precision instrument convinced me!

This set me thinking. Am I . . . exerting "pressure" on the scene around me—a pressure measurable not by ordinary means, but real? My very little strength may seem not worth trying to exert. But not all that happens is visible to human eyes.[2]

---

[2] F. W. Schwartz, Keswick "Daily Readings" calendar, 6 May 1976.

I have a section in my notebook called "disciples." At the top of the first page I wrote two years ago, "Father, please: one hundred disciples in my lifetime?" And in parentheses I put "four a year for twenty-five years?" That seemed a reasonable request. I was fifty at the time; that would be from fifty to seventy-five, and I'd still have a remainder of ten years to goof off while still ministering with Ray!

I've had twenty-three disciples these last six years, but they were scanty at first and have increased to about eight a year, so I would think, God willing, I can affect hundreds at close range before I die. And besides, if anyone is still asking me I'm not going to say "no" after I'm seventy-five!

At the top of my "disciples" page are several Scriptures I've jotted down while praying over this aspect of my life. One is John 17:19: "For their sakes I sanctify Myself, that they themselves also may be sanctified in truth." I dedicate myself to this; I set myself apart from lesser pursuits.

Also I've written 2 Corinthians 12:15a: "I will most gladly spend and be expended for your souls."

How precious is this attitude of Paul's—and doubtless of thousands of other Christians through the centuries! I want it to be my attitude, too.

I've kept a list of the twenty-three women I've counted as disciples. With some I've taken the initiative; especially when I've led them to know the Lord myself, then I say, "Hey, how would you like to get together once a week for some Bible study and prayer?" Some have come to me and asked, "Would you pray about discipling me for a while?"

On my notebook list of disciples I enter the date we first got together, and the date we terminated.

The first two were failures. Probably it was my fault; I just didn't know how to disciple well enough. I introduced them both to Christ, and I still believe their conversions were genuine. One met with me weekly for seven months and the other for nine months. Both drifted away because of being distracted over husbands with problems.

But I see from John 6:66 that Jesus himself lost some disciples, so apparently that doesn't make me a failure! I've found that if some fall away, there are always others near at hand ready to pick up the ball and run with it! So we're not to lose heart, but just learn from our mistakes and keep on with God's business.

The other twenty-one are all in good shape. In the early years of discipling (1970–1974) I never thought of cutoff dates; we met until there was a mutual agreement that the woman was ready to turn around, form her own group, and disciple as she had been discipled.

More recently we're apt to say, "Let's meet for six months," "over the summer," "from September to June"—something like that. A cutoff date makes it easier to start; you don't feel you're getting caught in a lifetime thing, like proposing marriage. Then instead of eventually petering out, you may decide to extend your time together. Or else, more likely, you end strongly and then multiply by dividing!

Year before last eight of us met together from September to June, and in June we made a date for a luncheon the next October when we would report what had happened to us since. The eight had grown to fifty-one!

I had a beautiful letter recently from a woman in the Washington, D.C. area after I had spoken there, saying, "My question is, just what do you *do* when you disciple women?" Well, dear friend, let me give you here all the guidelines I can, although that's a little like asking "What do you *do* when you raise children?" You follow a few basic rules, but then you find your own style and spend your life at it. You know that what you *are* in your life in Christ will have a greater effect than what you say or do.

Basic guidelines? Well, let's answer the question first of how you get together. You don't divide up a church membership by the alphabet or by neighborhoods and post the groups on a bulletin board. Your chemistry may not mix! This is something that becomes dreary and ponderous if it's administrated and watchdogged from above.

No, it must spring from the grass roots. People motivated by the desire to live obedient, biblical life styles just say to people they feel would be responsive, "What do you say we get together for a few months?"

But how do you find a leader? Well, obviously, if this is a true discipling situation (which we all need to be involved in), the leader is automatic. The discipling process needs to be a continual flow through every believer's life: you must be continually learning from someone who knows more than you do, and then (don't be the dead end!) you must be continually passing on what you know to someone who knows less. You say you don't know much? If all you know is John 3:16, get together with a nonchurch neighbor, have a cup of coffee, and tell her about it. Then if she says, "Hey, this was great; let's do it again next week," you've got one week to learn something new to tell her. Discipling is a wonderfully stretching experience!

But besides discipling groups, there's another kind of discipling, in which peers meet before the Lord. You might call it a "supportive fellowship." This is such a wonderful experience, you probably need both kinds of groups in your life. Here those who want to, take turns leading, and the idea is "where you're strong and I'm weak, you help me. Where I'm strong and you're weak, I'll help you. We'll all learn about Jesus from each other."

How often do you meet? Well, you meet together regularly, probably weekly, although I know many teen-agers and businessmen who also check in by telephone daily. Have the feeling, though, that this is not a meeting, it's a relationship. That means you're on call twenty-four hours a day, seven days a week.

How many meet? Occasionally God has guided me to a one-on-one relationship, but usually it's a better use of time to say that whatever you're sharing with one could be shared with perhaps four. At Lake Avenue Congregational Church, where we have hundreds of small groups, we've found by trial and error that groups can be four to eight. With more than eight you can begin to get anonymous; there's not time for the quiet ones to share their lives.

The meeting time must be systematic and structured so that it doesn't turn into a coffee klatsch. Four people will probably need 1–1½ hours weekly together; I'm in a group of four that needs 2–2½. Our group of eight last year found we needed two full hours without food; even then we barely made it.

But begin and end right on time, and follow an agenda so that everything gets included that you want to include.

This is not a Bible study, but it must include God's Word— enough of it for your life situations to spring out of it. No book studies, no filling in blanks! It's not primarily for information. Your adult Sunday School classes and other Bible classes provide that.

This is not a prayer meeting, but it must include prayer. Sometimes more, sometimes less. Vary the pattern, vary the format for freshness.

This is not a worship service, but it must include worship. Every time you gather in Jesus' name you must spend part of your time focusing on him alone. You can worship him in prayer. You can sing to him, or read together the words of worship hymns. Pray psalms to him. Talk of his attributes. Use your sanctified ingenuity!

This is not a sensitivity group, but it must include sharing. Don't let the sharing swallow up the whole time! Not often should it come first; we all are too prone to forget time when we talk about ourselves. Still, sharing is a crucial part, and needs special consideration.

Some people are afraid to get into small groups because they fear getting trapped into a confession session. Boy, so do I! Is it "airing dirty linen"? Count me out! And yet with our hundreds of small groups in our church over many years, I have yet, even once, to ever hear this mentioned as a problem.

You see, when you meet *in Jesus' name,* he is in the midst!
And his Holy Spirit is a gentleman! When he is in charge,
everything will be seemly and proper. Your group is not to be
problem-centered, but Christ-centered!

The first few weeks or months you probably will stick
pretty closely to worship, to the Scriptures, to prayer, to more
surface issues of your lives. Fine. Don't worry. Don't force
anything. The layers come off gradually, in an atmosphere
of holy love and growing acceptance.

Plenty of things will never be exposed. There are things in
my past I wouldn't tell anybody; why should I? God has forgiven and forgotten them. The point of a small group is to
lift, to encourage, to edify, to "strengthen one another in
God," as Jonathan did David.

The last essential ingredient of a group is accountability
for, and responsibility to, each other. Setting and sharing
goals helps here. If you know your sister's highest dreams and
longings, you know her better, and you know how to pray
for her. And when she knows yours, you have put yourself on
the line to be accountable. As a functioning sister she should
say to you from time to time, "How are you doing? How is
your quiet time coming? Have you been able to witness to
Gladys, your neighbor?" Submission in the Body of Christ
includes vulnerability, but that's what moves us all along
faster in our spiritual progress.

One more question: do you mix the sexes? Not for discipling. Titus 2:3–5 spells out, for instance, that "older women
[I would think spiritually older, most often] are to . . .
encourage the young women to love their husbands, to love
their children, to be sensible, pure, workers at home, kind,
being subject to their own husbands, that the word of God
may not be dishonored." (You see what I mean? This type of
thing isn't a Bible class, though you need that elsewhere; it's
giving and getting help in life situations.)

You may not want to mix the sexes in a supportive fellowship, either. Our men tell us that when they meet as brothers and want to learn from each other how to love and lead their wives, they'd feel pretty inhibited if the wife were sitting there in the group. The opposite is also certainly true. Women have women-situations, and they need to be alone to dig deep into them. But I try to mix single and married women in my groups; both need the other and are so much the richer for it!

Couples' groups serve a different purpose, and they're wonderful. Ray and I give every Thursday night to four other couples, and how precious they are to us! We've gone through deep waters together—fasted for each other's children, prayed through financial temptations. All the couples, at some time or other, have taken planes home early from out of town to be together, and the men have frequently gone without dinner, when business ran late, in order to be there. We've even phoned each other on Thursday nights from different states, three couples on one end of the line and two couples on the other, though normally we're right in Pasadena when Thursday comes.

That's commitment! It speaks louder than words.

When I had the hysterectomy a few months ago I missed the Thursday I was in the hospital, but the following one I was home. So they met in our living room (I had to insist; they thought it would be too hard on me). I put on my best nightie and robe, and it was one of the sweetest times we've ever had. God is so good!

We had a sad letter recently from a couple of missionary "dropouts." They are dear friends of ours and wonderful people. The letter began, "We're home!" and went on to explain:

There seemed to be no spiritual side to our work or our lives. We were living in spiritual isolation—no fellowship with other Christians, local or missionaries. The lack of the spiritual side to the work made the name "missionary" uncomfortable. The lack of spiritual fellowship with other Christians made it impossible.

All in all, coming home seemed the best thing to do, and here we are.

I think in their place we would have come home, too. God didn't make any of us to be Lone Rangers, riding off into the sunset jangling our silver bullets. He constructed us so that we're lonely unless we have firm, deep fellowship with him and with other believers. Not even God himself is a loner; he's a Trinity, and he commands us to get deep into him and into each other.

Dear Christian friend, when your life is all over, what will it all have been about? For what will you be judged? I used to read 1 Corinthians 3 and think that all the stuff about wood-hay-stubble versus gold-silver-precious stones referred to the quality of life we'd lived, and how we'll be judged for that. Then I woke up to the context of that passage. Paul has been talking about himself and Apollos, another discipler, and he says in verse 9, "[Apollos and I] are God's fellow-workers; you [Christians] are . . . God's building."

Then he begins to show that once the foundation of Christ has been laid, men build upon that foundation the superstructure of the church, the temple of God. Each person they add to the church is one more stone in the building. But they'll be judged for the quality of the stones that they add—"the quality of each man's work," the quality of Christians they add to the church of God!

At the end, fire judges it all. The wood, hay, stubble—some Christians' work during their lives—will burn up, but they themselves will be saved, just barely making it into heaven, the smell of fire on their clothes (v. 15). But those who discipled carefully and well, who built quality Christians into the church—these will receive a reward.

And that's how a Christian's life will be judged—by the quality of his (or her) "ministry."

Lord, how precious to me are the names on my "disciples" page! You say the test of fire shows whether or not they remain. Oh, keep me faithfully loving and teaching and sympathizing and empathizing and interceding, that my work may remain. . . .

I have to tell you one more story. Number sixteen on my list is "Nels Ortlund," the only male! Beside his name is May 27, 1975, and no terminating date.

I can't tell you how much fun this little eleven-year-old son of ours is. He's going to be some kind of tiger when he's grown—and that's the kind of children we love to raise. Aggressive? This little fellow is there first with the most.

At his last annual medical checkup the nurse was doing the preliminaries—weighing, measuring, asking questions.

"How is he sleeping?" she said.

Nels piped up, "I sleep very well." She wrote that down.

"How's his appetite, Mrs. Ortlund?"

"I eat everything," said Nels. She wrote that down.

"Mrs. Ortlund," she asked me, "how are his bowels?"

Nels was in there again first, trying to be helpful: "*A, e, i, o, u,*" he said. . . .

The nurse was still barely under control when she left the room five minutes later.

Well, that wasn't the story I started to tell you.

The evening of last May 26 Nels had been a very bad boy. He was so naughty I spanked him, and Ray spanked him, and I cried, and Ray cried, and Nels cried. It was the crisis of his ten-year-old life! When he was finally in bed and we shut the door, we could still hear him sniffling out loud, "God, I don't know why I was so dumb. I'll never do that again; I'll never, never!"

The next day he came to me and said, "Mother, you disciple all those ladies; will you disciple me?" What a tender moment! The two of us bought him a notebook like mine. We decided to meet daily at breakfast. (Ray is always out on business or prayer breakfasts.) And we'd start out reading about Daniel—a real "he-man" teen-ager who dared to stand alone for God, who prayed every day, and who took care of his body and ate the right foods and so on.

I shared with him my goals, for him to pray over and help me, and he made four for me to help him with. By his birthday, October 15, he wanted

1. His temper cooled down
2. To get acquainted with new friends at summer camp
3. To know Daniel thoroughly by then
4. To eat some green vegetable and some fruit every day (He called that his "Daniel diet.")

He's been doing great ever since!

And it has made me realize the vast difference between seeing our children just as our children and seeing them as our disciples—our obvious, number one, built-in disciples. If they're just our children, then our only concerns are the concerns of any worldly mother: to feed and clothe them, get them into the right schools, well married, etc. But if they're also our disciples, then, more than anyone else, within those twenty or so precious years we have them, we're to teach them everything Jesus has taught us.

We don't deserve the children we have. We did a lot of things wrong. But here's a letter from Margie, our second daughter, written ten years ago when she was away in college. It still brings tears to my eyes, and if we had a fire it would be one of those things I'd grab first:

Dearest parents,

I felt compelled this afternoon to write this after a big wave came over me of love and gratitude for you both, mingled with a twinge of homesickness. I felt a little bogged down with soon-coming decisions that will have to be made, and my first impulse was to talk to you, and get your advice. Then I felt frustrated that I couldn't. And then I felt so grateful that that *was* my first impulse. And you've made that to be true. Because of your wise patience and obvious love and understanding, it is very natural for me to turn to you. That's unusual for a college girl, sadly so. I couldn't be more blessed to have you as parents. I can feel confident that I will always be happy, content, and will have a happy home, because this is my heritage and all that I know. I have models to follow: one is for a wife and mother in you, dear Mother; another is for a husband—I know what I want when I see the type of man you are, Daddy; and the third in a home, for I've never been confronted with a happier and more exciting one. My heart wells with thanksgiving to God for His goodness to me. And you're a big hunk of that goodness!

So thank you for being so wonderful and open to me in my childishness, inconsistencies, and stupidity. (But I'm learning!)

Much love,
Margie

The sequel to this is that now she's married to a wonderful pastor, and is the happy mother of three.

No, we don't deserve them. But we're to teach them everything Jesus has taught us. "And lo," says Jesus as we do it, "*I am with you always*" (Matt. 28:20, emphasis mine).

10. *Your Public Life*

There are two kinds of personalities in this world, and you are one of the two. People can tell which, as soon as you walk into a room: your attitude says either "Here I am," or "There you are."

Which kind are you?

Let's back up and recap the book so far. At the center of your life must be God in Jesus Christ. There the ultimate issues are settled, and you can start living from the inside out.

Your person is part of the center, too; your body is the flesh that clothes his Presence. Fantastic thought! So your looks are important, before him, and representing him.

Your long-term goals set the course of where you want to go, under his plans. Your short-term goals keep redirecting you to stay on course, and your daily scheduling is the discipline to get you there, with God's glory and rewards when it's over. Goals and scheduling take time—quiet time—and are part of your life behind the scenes.

Moving out from that central core of you, you push aside a filmy gauze curtain to your immediate surroundings, which you share with no one or a very few: your bedroom, bath, closets . . . we'll conclude with desk and notebook.

Within that concentric circle are people—perhaps a husband, perhaps a roommate, perhaps children . . . and others. There are enough marriage books and human relationship books. There are enough child-raising books. This book is mostly to help you deal with the one thing you will be all your adult life: yourself as a woman.

As a woman your eternity-oriented task is to affect others, to move them to God through the Savior, Jesus Christ. Your temporary task, for the years you have them, is to affect the members of your physical family, by whatever means you can, to be "born again" into God's eternal family and to grow within that family to spiritual maturity. Your lifelong task, at least from conversion on, whether married or single, is to influence everyone you can, by whatever means you can, to the same ends—to help them become temple material of gold, silver, and precious stones.

The ways you'll do this are as varied as God's creative powers allow, which are infinite. He never stamps out cookie-cutter Christians.

Now we're moving out from the middle to the edges of your life. But where are the edges? Lines and shades blur. The more God-integrated and focused your central core is, the more powerful is the push outward, until (only God knows) your public life may become public indeed. At least it will be as far as eternity is concerned.

When you read the chapter title "Your Public Life," you may have thought you have no public life at all. But you certainly do. Beyond your most intimately known circle of people, what lives do you touch? Who knows you? Many at your church, and perhaps in other organizations. The grocer, the bank teller, the postman, your neighbors—are you not just touching their lives, but influencing them for Jesus?

> Only one life; 'twill soon be past;
> Only what's done for Christ will last!

Walk out that door of your home to your job, or whatever your world may be, saying, "There you are! There are all you precious people, with feeling and needs. Who of you is ready today to be pressured to God, gently or strongly, as he leads me?"

Let me tell you a visual way I see this happen. I know a Hawaiian woman who strings a number of leis early each Sunday morning, not for anyone in particular! Then she comes to church praying, "Lord, who needs my leis today? A newcomer? Someone discouraged? Lead me to the right people."

That's emerging into public life saying, "There you are!"

Your public life should flow out of your private life. How important your outward direction is! You represent Christ. Hold your head up, as Psalm 3:3 tells you to. Plan your shampoos so that you don't go to the grocery store in rollers. Switch purses—it's worth the time—so that you coordinate when you go out. Compliment the friend you're meeting for lunch by looking like God's woman. Gideon was known by his appearance and clothing to be a leader among men (Judg. 8:18); so should you!

Look quality—and think quality. It will tell on your face if you obey Philippians 4:8, letting your mind dwell on that which is true, honorable, right, pure, lovely, and so on! It will help that lovely woman you long to be grow as you practice God's presence in public, keeping a running conversation going with him: "Lord, bless that man walking toward me; Father, help me to be a wise, careful driver; God, I love you. . . ." Discipline yourself to bring "every thought captive to the obedience of Christ" (2 Cor. 10:5).

Look quality, think quality—talk quality. It frightens me, how many of the New Testament references to woman have to do with the problems of her tongue! There are plenty of books on all sides of the women's liberation movement, but let me just remind both you and me that it was Eve who

sinned first and not Adam (1 Tim. 2:14), so let's conduct
ourselves with care, and caution.

Have you a boss over you at your work? Give him the
deference the Scriptures command (1 Pet. 13–20).

Have you people who work under you? In your most
feminine way, "boss well." God will give you all the resources
you need to be wise, to be firm, to handle people with authority, and yet like Teddy Roosevelt to speak softly!

(Incidentally, regarding the tongue, have you noticed that
because some areas of humor are off-limits to Christians, a
few of them think what's really racy is bathroom jokes? As
Casey Stengel used to say, "Include me out.")

Look quality, think quality, talk quality—and expose yourself to quality. In your entertainment and social life, watch
what feeds your mind. Our computer-expert friends talk about
GIGO—"Garbage In, Garbage Out." I don't know how you
feel about it, but of the few PG movies I've seen, most were
such garbage that I'm sorry I exposed my mind and heart to
them. Don't get insensitive; don't get used to garbage. What
goes in will come out; pretty soon we'll smell.

Once in a while you may get caught in something not of
your own choosing. Well, you can't stop birds from lighting
on your head, but you can keep them from making a nest
in your hair.

One way of keeping your public life wholesome is by seeing
that your larger circle of friends, as well as your intimate
circle, are godly people.

Ray and I went to a fantastic dinner party one evening.
Dave and Jackie, the host and hostess, live in an elegant home
so we dressed appropriately. We had been briefed that the
rule for the occasion was that all the conversation must praise
God. The whole evening was both hilarious and spectacular,
but what I remember most was sitting on our high-backed
chairs in that baronial dining room as Jackie described the
first week of her life as a Christian—a week of straight Bible

reading, chain smoking, and tears. We laughed, we cried, we were lifted.

The Bible has a lot to say about how to treat the larger circle of our Christian family. 1 Timothy 5:1–2 says it well in *The Living Bible:* "Never speak sharply to an older man, but plead with him respectfully just as though he were your own father. Talk to the younger men as you would to much loved brothers. Treat the older women as mothers, and the girls as your sisters, thinking only pure thoughts about them" (written to a fellow). And again, *The Living Bible* in 1 Peter 3:8: "You should be like one big happy family, full of sympathy toward each other, loving one another with tender hearts and humble minds."

There's no flirting here. The relationships may be precious indeed between spiritual brothers and sisters, even to greeting one another "with a holy kiss" (2 Cor. 13:12)—in this case a peck on the cheek—but God's Holy Spirit guides always what is affirming and encouraging in Christ without going any further. Love in the Body of Christ is sensitive love. On the one hand, if you're a wife, it "is not jealous," or easily "provoked" (1 Cor. 13:4–5). On the other hand, if you're the nonwife, it "does not act unbecomingly" (1 Cor. 13:5).

In the matter of marital status we have to be absolutely loose, satisfied with what we are. Are you bound to a husband? Don't seek to be released. Are you single? Don't seek a husband (1 Cor. 7:27). These are hard things to say in a corrupt society which pressures us women either to marry, or, more recently, to be swinging singles. Often the married ones long for freedom, and the singles fight the "swinging" image and long for a husband. Paul talks long and deeply about this in 1 Corinthians 7; read it carefully. He seems to say, in essence:

1. In troubled times, you're really better off being single—free to please only God.
2. If you do marry, you haven't sinned; but be warned: it's

not easy to have the necessary double allegiance of pleasing both God and a husband.

3. Because time is so short, and the present form of this world is passing away: if you have a husband, love him and obey him, but—easy does it. Live for eternity. Live for God. Don't be possessed, don't be entangled, until you're only a wife, nothing more.

Concerning sex he says, "If you're married, enjoy sex regularly, faithfully! Your body belongs to your husband." And "If you're not married, God will either give you control or give you a husband!"

I point you to these Scriptures as a wife who is deeply, joyfully in love. Why shouldn't I be? I'm spoiled to death with such a treasure of a blond, beautiful, godly husband, and I know with total certainty that I'm his sweetheart, and he is mine. Still, both of us have to be loose enough in our possession of each other that the loss of one of us wouldn't destroy the other.

"For me, to live is Christ," not Ray. Into God's hands I commend my spirit, and my life, and all I am. He can give, he can take away, his name will still be "Blessed." God will keep in perfect peace the mind which is stayed on him, himself.

The last thing to say about your public life is: make it very public! You've already made the decision to disciple chosen ones behind the scenes, and you've proportioned your lifestyle to give them a meaningful chunk of your time.

So don't cling to them in public as well. Reach out! Socialize. Stretch out your heart to know many who are different from you—richer, poorer, or whatever. Make your circle of this broader, necessarily shallower love as large as possible.

Be sure that you have nothing against any other believer, that all the lines of communication are open and clear (Matt. 5:23–24). Then once that's settled, be a "baby-kissing politician"! Touch is wonderful; reach when you pass people to grab a hand, touch a shoulder.

On this earth you will probably never know them all, but affect all the lives you can. "Behold how those Christians love one another," they said in the first century. And of the ones who aren't believers—your warmth, your smile may open doors which will draw them in.

"There you are," you say to your public world. "God loves you, and I love you. What can I do for you today?"

And from that well-tended, precious center of you, the circle will enlarge . . . and enlarge . . . and enlarge.

11.   *Your Desk*

I've saved for close to the end of this book your desk and your notebook. They're the two means of putting you all together, tying you up in a package with a pink ribbon. (Salmon? Black and white?)

The philosophies of life have to be right, first. Then you're ready to house the tools needed to carry out the philosophies.

My particular desk is like me: it's still in process. I dream of a lovely one, with built-in shelves and cupboards on the adjoining wall—the total look both efficient and feminine, but leaning slightly more to the feminine. Well, one of these days! It's not on the financial agenda yet.

In the meantime, I have a door laid over two-drawer filing cabinets. It's in a light, airy corner of our pale blue and green, fifteen-by-thirty-foot master bedroom, and the door (let's say desk top) and chair are painted pale blue, matching the woodwork. The chair arms are a shade too high for the desk top, and from being shoved under, some paint has come off each arm. Well, as I say, I'm not yet what I'm going to be, either.

Over the desk hangs a large photograph of Ray, taken by

and framed in exquisite blue velvet by our artistic, loving son, Bud. Ray and Bud had been attending the Lausanne Congress on Evangelism in Switzerland, and one afternoon sat beside Lake Lucerne praying together. As they finished prayer Ray turned his face away to look over the lake—and Bud snapped the picture.

Under the picture is a pale blue plaque of Psalm 34:3, the words Ray used when he proposed to me: "O magnify the Lord with me, and let us exalt His Name together!"

On the desk are pale blue appointment books and matching telephone, and a few other sentimental treasures.

A "Week-at-a-Glance" notebook is central, containing social appointments and telephone numbers. It lies open to the day. As soon as appointments are made by phone they go into my "Week-at-a-Glance." Then if they're within the next three months, they're transcribed to the "to do" section of the notebook that goes everywhere with me.

White wicker desk organizers hold note paper, business envelopes, post cards, and stamps. A small bookrack holds several Bibles, a dictionary, and a few books I'm reading at the moment. A white onyx dish from my friend Myrtle holds paper clips and rubber bands. Blue velvet containers from my sister Margie hold pens and pencils, Scotch tape, scissors—you know—and letters to be answered. The large matching lamps are special, because they've been with us since our early-poor days when they flanked the living room sofa.

The left bottom file drawer holds original manuscripts of all the books Ray and I have written so far, plus file folders of material for future books, into which we continually drop new quotations and ideas.

The left top file drawer holds financial information: a folder for bills, another for receipts, another for bank books and information. It holds boxes of extra blank checks, and it holds a three-by-five-inch index card file box of Christmas card addresses. Then there's room for supplies of typing paper, scribbling tablets, and music manuscript paper.

There's a large brown leather notebook initialed in gold in which I do my writing; it was a gift from our loving choir when I substituted at the organ for a while.

In the bottom right drawer I've filed all correspondence with music publishers and SESAC, my composers' affiliation; all copyright certificates; and copies of all my published and unpublished music works. That one is stuffed to overflowing! Either I quit writing music or reorganize for more file space.

So far, you probably relate to drawer two, but not to one or three. Never mind, you have your own special interests. I didn't even mention that for years I've torn pictures I loved out of decorating magazines, and they're also filed away, under "bathrooms," "bedrooms," "breakfast rooms," et cetera—for ideas when we redecorate, or just for occasional perusing while in a warm tub.

But drawer four—to this one you must relate. This top right drawer I set up after reading Ernest Dimnet's *The Art of Thinking*, which for me was a terrific motivator.

The first section of the drawer is file folders from *A* to *Z* just to put things in, so I'll know where they are! Since Dimnet, I never—well, hardly ever—set anything I must do something about soon, or someday, on a vacant spot somewhere. (Then, when "soon" or "someday" comes, under which pile of accumulation did I put that whatzit?) No, I think of the word with which I'd most likely associate it, and I drop it into the alphabetical file. If I need to be reminded about it, I jot that onto the right calendar day in my notebook. And when I want it I can put my finger right on it.

C holds concert tickets, mail order catalogs.

D holds unused Disneyland tickets!

G holds all those little guarantee slips for the household appliances and other things with dated guarantees.

I holds our insurance information.

L holds our "Let's Dine Out" cards.

S holds the correspondence on my future speaking dates and Nels's school information.

Well, you get the idea!

Behind that alphabetical file is another *A* to *Z* series of folders. These are my own Bible studies or sermon notes or ideas on any subjects I want to file and pursue. I find I've stashed away, for instance, things on the Bible, on family, on the Holy Spirit, on marriage and, among other things, on "self-image." (I think it's often being taught erroneously, and I toss into the folder Scriptures I find on that subject, to study one of these days.)

Behind that file is another series of folders marked from Genesis to Revelation. Anything anyone teaches me from one of the books of Scripture, or anything I study on my own, I drop into the file. But the accumulation of Bible truths grows; I've got lots of things I can pass along when I have an opportunity.

I think of all the years and years I studied or read the Bible without writing anything down. I must have forgotten tons of wonderful stuff. The Lord was patient to keep teaching me anything new.

I was talking about this to 400 women at a conference recently, trying to explain how my filing system works.

"Suppose Ray's been preaching a series on Christ our Wisdom from the Book of Proverbs," I said. "When the series is done, I drop all my notes into the Proverbs file. There they are, in my own words, the way I understood it, ready to pass on to others.

"Or suppose I've studied the creation in Genesis; I drop all my notes into the Genesis file. Or, say, the miracles of the Gospel of John—I drop them all into the John."

I began to feel the place rock and reel.

"File!" I shouted. "The John file!"

Sometimes the Lord has to scrape my talks off the floor, the walls, and the ceiling, and put them back together again.

Remember, Jesus said to you and me in Matthew 28:19–20, "Go therefore and make disciples, . . . teaching them to observe all that I commanded you." Perhaps you'll someday be a gifted, important Bible teacher in front of huge classes; perhaps you won't. But if you take Matthew 28:19–20 seriously, you need some system for accumulating what Jesus is telling you, so that you can make disciples, at least one-on-one over cups of coffee, and teach them what you've learned.

There's your desk, large or small, my friend. Put it together to work for you. Make it your servant, to respond with what you want immediately, at the touch of a finger. Make it sleek and uncluttered. Make it pretty and feminine.

Mostly, make it a tool to help you live a life of obedience to God and effectiveness with people.

12.   Your Notebook

Last year I spoke to a luscious-looking crowd of 150 women gathered for a one-day mini-retreat at the La Canada Country Club. I talked to them in the afternoon about what a notebook could do for their lives.

The next day, noticing I was nearly out of filler paper for my own, I dropped into the local stationer's store.

"I don't have any," said the manager. "I don't know what's happened. We've had a run on it like you wouldn't believe, just yesterday and this morning. And not just paper, but the binders, dividers, calendar pages—everything." He scratched his head.

"Well," I grinned, "you just ought to plan better."

And the letters keep coming in:

"Because of you, I now carry a notebook. . . ."

"Your suggestions for a notebook . . . have been such a blessing to me. . . ."

"I began a notebook . . . and don't see how I ever got along without it! I have many different sections now, such as songs, books and tapes lent and borrowed. . . ."

"Thanks for the much needed shot in the arm. . . ."

Wherever I go, beautiful, motivated women bounce up to

me hugging their notebooks. The brunettes have black ones, the redheads carry brown, the blondes have navy. They've heard me speak somewhere.

I can't believe it, either. I, too, scratch my head.

When I first bought a notebook and organized it into sections, no one had suggested it to me. I didn't do it because it was going to be some great new beginning in my life. I can't even remember actually getting it.

Over the ensuing months I began leaning on my notebook more and more for daily living, seeing what it could do. Fortunately it was brown and just Bible-size, so it was easy to get the habit of going out the door with Bible, notebook, and purse.

After several years of literally living out of it, hesitantly, very hesitantly, I shared it one time at a women's conference. Whammo! It went off like a bombshell. Scores told me they were going home to buy notebooks. I shared it at other conferences, and the feedback began. I'd hear the words "It's changed my life."

Even so, I was fearful of speaking about it. Opening up my notebook was opening up *me*. Why wouldn't they think I was on an ego trip? Why would they be built up in the faith by hearing about my Bible studies with Nels, the building of my wardrobe, my occasional struggles over merging my heart with Ray's or over finances, the pouring of my life into disciples, my goals, my devotions?

Well, I've already shared with you my reticence about this. In early conferences I always said, "Now, this part of my speaking is so personal, I'd prefer no taping." But as the blessing grew and I realized my life on the altar was being used, I threw caution out the window and let it all be taped. And here I am, putting it in a book.

So my notebook is 7″ x 9″, three-ringed, and holds paper 5½″ x 8½″. That's a comfortable size to rest with my Bible on my left arm, with my purse hanging from a strap. For all of us women, that's simple. We've typed whole pages while talking and cradling a phone on our shoulder, or cooked three-course dinners with a baby on one hip.

Now, as I tell you what's in my notebook, remember that yours won't be identical. I'll just share mine to give you ideas, and your notebook will become a reflection of your own individual life.

The first section of my notebook is my calendar pages, torn out as each day ends, so that when I flip open my notebook I'm looking at "today." These days in Hawaii are gloriously empty, but today includes a thing or two: wire congratulations to Joan and Marv on their twenty-fifth anniversary. More stamps for post cards. Ho, hum!

(Actually, the schedule of this month has been: up at 8:30; leave house at 9:30; brunch out with Ray and Nels; to the beach where Nels plays, Ray plays, prays, studies and writes, and I sit in the shade and have devotions and then write. End of afternoon home to change clothes, out to a great dinner and occasional entertainment, usually home to early bed. One day a week we break the routine and sightsee or cavort together all day.)

The first day after return home says 8:45 hair tint (after a month, I'll need it), deposit paycheck, write and mail bills, electric blanket ready to pick up at laundry, etc.—a quick slip back into routine.

The important thing about your "to do" section is to have your notebook forever with you. When you think of something you need to do, a shopping item to buy, jot it down immediately *on the day when you intend to do it, or buy it.* If someone asks you for a date, you'll always know if you're available or not.

"I'd love to have a copy of that song," says a lady at church. In my notebook I jot down on the following Sunday's page to bring her one.

I leave off shoes for repair. "They'll be ready Friday," the man says. I flip open to Friday and write "shoes." I clip the claim check to the page.

If you keep your notebook with you, to write everything and then read everything, you'll never forget anything again! That's a promise.

(I don't see how any woman who's had a hysterectomy could ever live without the "to do" section of a notebook. Some pages of the month say "One pill." Some say "Two pills." Some say "No pill." I don't know what would happen if I ever got them mixed up. I don't dare ask. Maybe I'd grow a beard.)

One woman wrote recently, "To say the least, I can't tell you how much I've received, as so much of it has become such a part of my life I can't remember when I wasn't carrying around my notebook, jotting my whole life down everywhere I go."

What are the jobs you hate? Write them in on different days; spread them out! But put them in your notebook: clean the oven, face a sister about a ticklish issue. It will overcome your habit of procrastination and give you a great sense of quiet accomplishment.

Write in your time with God every single day, when it realistically fits your schedule that day. It may be at a different time every day, but it will be there because you deliberately planned for it and saw to it that it happened. It is priority number one in your life, no matter what else goes on!

One characteristic of a good driver is that he always looks ahead half a block or so; he anticipates. So with a good *liver* (what a word!); you live glancing ahead half a week or more to know where you're going.

Then each evening take a good look at the following day. Decide what you'll wear: hang it out, or jot it down. (Shoes polished? Everything ready?) Chart your course from first to last item, particularly if it's an errand day. It will save you time and gas. Number the items from first to least importance; if some don't get done you can rewrite them on a future day. What do you need to take with you? Pile them together in a handy spot: the book back to the library, the china cup to be mended. Pray over the events of the day, the people you'll see. You'll sleep easier, and the next morning you won't spin your wheels getting going.

As the day advances cross off the items. At the end of the day rewrite what you didn't get done, thank the Lord for it all, and throw the page away.

The first divider in my notebook says "goals" on it. I shared them with you in chapter five, and now I'll tell you what I prayed on paper after I wrote the goals. (You'll have to believe me; I never dreamed when I wrote these words that anyone but God would see them!)

> Father, I want to pour my life increasingly into You, into people, and into work. [Those are the "three priorities," as you recognize.] Oh, may I be so submerged in Yourself, in Your Word and in prayer that my personality will be oiled by the Holy Spirit.
>
> I want to be sweet, gracious, thoughtful, hospitable—working hard behind the scenes without seeming pressured.
>
> I want to relax and play with Ray when he needs me; give us fun dates together; make me fun to be with. For Nels, too, Lord.
>
> Make my hair, figure, make-up, and clothes right, Lord, so they'll be proud of me.
>
> Help me to write music for You, Lord—songs, hymns, and anthems that will meet the needs of the Body.
>
> Help me to complete our house, inside and out, without being consumed by it.
>
> Thanks, Father, thanks!

I don't know what your dreams and visions are. I only know that God has them for you, so you need to get away, if you don't know, and commune with him and find out. Be specific; make your goals as measurable as you can, so you'll know if you're making them or not! This is absolutely crucial before you strike out on your own in some new direction not of God's leading.

And don't clean out your closet before you make goals. Remember, the sculptor deals with the large mass first. Details come later.

At the back of this notebook section are other miscellaneous goals. House goals: as God wills, complete my desk area, repaint the downstairs, re-cover living room furniture, etc. Financial goals: finish paying back our life insurance loan, increase our savings accounts. I notice jotted in between things,

> Take from our lives the strain and stress,
> And let our ordered lives confess
> The beauties of Thy peace.[1]

Well, your notebook is just your personal thing! Put in it whatever you please.

Another page, my wardrobe: a list of my current outfits, with accessories, jewelry, etc. Another page, my exercise goals: in my stair climbing I've worked up gradually from ten round trips to 72 each morning and 60 each evening.

You'll probably have plenty of other projects and interesting side trips in life to record with your goals. They'll be as varied and as wonderful as all God's beautiful women in this world!

My next notebook section is for Bible study. Pasted onto the first page is a chronological outline of the books of the Old and New Testaments, so I can remember what goes where. Then comes the study I happen to be doing at the moment, principles of leadership. I started with the lives of Moses and Aaron, reading from Exodus 2, and so far I've gotten to

---

[1] John Greenleaf Whittier. "Dear Lord and Father of Mankind."

Judges 9:55, just jotting down beside each reference principles as I see them. Pretty soon I'll quit that and drop them into the Bible study file in my desk, under *L* for "Leadership!"

You may be a long-time Bible scholar or a brand-new beginner, but you can begin writing something as you study each day. He'll help you; he'll put an idea in your head, and another idea months from now, and by ten years—dozens and dozens! How rich your storehouse will be, and it will all be yours! Get going in the study of God's Word!

The next section of my notebook is called "disciples," with the list I told you about in chapter nine. The list is in ink, and at the bottom of the page in light pencil are those who've asked recently if they can join me for a while. So I've written in my "to do" section, on August 3, "Pray over disciples for fall." Well, Jesus did that, too, in Luke 6:12–16.

Also in the "disciples" section is a page of the thirty-nine members of a Wednesday morning Bible class I teach. They come from all churches, Protestant and Catholic, as well as from no church. What a dear, eager group they are! Recently we had a big splashy dinner together, adding husbands, boy friends, and friends, and there were eighty of us at Betty's house across the street. Then Dr. Ralph Byron, chief surgeon of the City of Hope and one of our Sunday School teachers at church, sketched the story of his life and how he'd met Jesus, for the benefit of lots of the guests who haven't yet. To use Ralph's favorite word, it was a sensational evening.

The next three notebook sections are titled "Nels," "neighbors," and "couples," and you can guess why. In Nels's section, we record each time we're together, what Scripture we read, one summarizing comment by him, and any other pertinent information. Some pretty astute words come out of his eleven-year-old mind, like the latest entry:

"It takes a while to learn a lesson, but there's no stopping God from getting through to you."

(When I think of Nels I always have to put in a little

extra. He's our favorite entertainment in these years of our lives. Recently Nels experienced his first major illness, a few weeks of infectious mononucleosis. The first week he was really sick, with a burning throat and a neck like mumps.

We went in to see the doctor for a gamma globulin shot. Oh, how they can hurt! Nels lay on his tummy as the shot went into his hip, and he never made a sound, but his face was contorted into the look of strong crying, and tears were streaming down his big-boy cheeks.

As he lay there trying to get his breath back, his eyes lighted on a Dr. Seuss book on the floor, *There's a Wocket in My Pocket.*

"There's some heat," Nels finally said, "in my seat.")

The "neighbors" are Beulah next-door on our south side, whose heart God opened two Januarys ago (we started meeting together weekly); Betty across the street, who accepted Christ and joined us in October of that year; and Doris, down the block, whom we prayed in shortly after. On page 1 are their names and birthdays (love has to be practical and thoughtful, right?), and then a prayer I wrote to God on behalf of each of them, expressing the visions and goals God had given me for each of their lives. Clipped to the back of the page are some sentimental treasures: written expressions of love from them, prayer requests that recall God's wonderful answers. Then each page notes our meeting date, at whose home, what we studied, what the prayer requests were, etc.

Recently one of the three made group goals for us, which the rest of us ratified:

1. Greater accountability
2. Check list for prayers and how answered
3. Outreach
   a. List names of people we know that need God's Word
   b. Work together, or as individuals, to reach them
4. Two weekends a year together
5. Attend one of Anne's conferences per year

6. Check our progress every three months
7. Wednesdays adhere to a time schedule. Homework often.

A lot of these goals indicate they're hungry to stretch and grow and that includes shaping up *me,* their leader. Good; that's just the kind of shove from behind I need, and I love them for it.

One page of this "neighbors" section of our notebooks is worth duplicating for this book, for you to copy if you like. It lists every way the New Testament mentions that members of the Body of Christ can communicate with other members. These are often repeated, but they boil down to thirteen ways, which we listed in a column. Then, as the months go by, each of us can see in how many scriptural ways we're communicating with each of the other three. I can see where I'm weak, and pray for new ways to help and encourage my dear sisters, as they help and encourage me. What we came up with is on the next page.

The "couples" section of my notebook, concerning Ray's and my Thursday night group with four other husbands and wives, has the same format. These sections become the records of our spiritual pilgrimages together, and they are precious indeed. As I look back six months and read what each one was praying for at that time, I marvel at how God has met our needs, answered our requests, and moved us along. He is magnificent! Children have been turned to Christ, large business ventures have been prayed into being; it's been some year together.

When I talk about putting lives together in small groups at conferences, afterward I get letters like this:

> When you spoke at the Women's Retreat at Mount Hermon, He used you in my life to awaken and burden me for a closer daily walk with Christ, by means of a small group. How anxious I was! And what a blessing it's been! I'm really learning to adore

	Betty	Beulah	Doris	Comments
Suffering together				
Rejoicing together				
Bearing one another's burdens				
Restoring one another				
Praying together				
Teaching, admonishing				
Refreshing one another				
Encouraging one another				
Forgiving one another				
Confessing to one another				
Being truthful with one another				
Stimulating one another to good deeds				
Giving to one another				

my Lord, praise Him, and give thanks. Accountability, and knowing I have five sisters who love me and are always available has made the way so much easier these past few months. I know God doesn't want us to go it alone.

No, dear woman whoever you are, he doesn't want me to, either. I've fallen on my face enough times by now to see how closely tied I must be to a few close-in brothers and sisters!

Another letter received recently says:

I want to share with you how successful the notebook idea has been in my life, and that I have initiated a five-gal prayer-and-share group, after much prayer myself. We all have read Ray's book,[2] and started our notebooks together, and what a closeness we already have and specific answers to prayer and such loving care for one another.

Already another group has formed through one of my friends, as I've shared the notebook idea with so many. . . . Something so simple has certainly got my life together so much more, and so many of my friends God has allowed me to influence for Him in this way.

Something funny before I close. My sister was waiting in her doctor's office recently and noticed an attractive lady across from her with a notebook and Bible just so busy and engrossed in her writing and reading. The nurse looked into the waiting room and called who would be next: Anne Ortlund! my sister . . . just couldn't believe it; the teacher actually practices what she preaches!

The next notebook section every Christian should have! I titled it "sermons," but it's for every time I hear teaching or preaching. Then my pen is ready, and I start writing notes as copiously and completely as I can. Particularly, I note all Scripture references. Every few weeks I transfer my note pages to the Bible study file in my desk, and at a moment's notice

---

[2] Raymond C. Ortlund, *Lord, Make My Life a Miracle* (Glendale, Cal.: Regal Books, 1975).

(almost) I've got material to pass on to others. It was somebody else's thoughts, but when I write it down for myself I
understand it, and it becomes mine to pass on.

I think about our daughter Sherry, and what a wealth of
scriptural knowledge she has. Last year when she was twenty-
eight a few college girls came to her and asked if she would
disciple them—since she was a "godly older woman"! "Think
of it, Mother," she complained to me in shocked tones. But
she gave them a wonderful year.

How was all this knowledge of the Word of God acquired?
Perhaps a major reason is that Sherry has taken notes on all
sermons since she was in junior high school.

And what a joy for a preacher to have people in front of
him taking notes! Otherwise, how can he tell if they're planning next week's menus or next year's vacation, or what? In
fact, it encourages the whole Body of Christ in worship together.

The last section of my notebook, "prayers," is the best of
all. How could it have taken me forty-two years of living the
Christian life before I ever started writing my prayers? I had
absolutely no idea what it was going to do for me.

Before, if you'd asked me what I'd prayed about three days
earlier, or maybe an hour earlier, unless it was something
crucial, I'd have no idea.

When I started writing prayers I just let the words flow on
paper the way they had done out of my mouth, putting down
both the important and the seemingly inconsequential. After
a few months when I started looking back over what I'd first
prayed, I was staggered to discover how seriously God had
taken my prayers! A sentence or two, just sort of thrown in,
had sometimes started the wheels of heaven turning until the
requests had ever-enlarging ramifications and affected ever-
enlarging numbers of people! I was learning such a lesson of
the power of prayer, it utterly shook me.

A letter from a woman confirmed another feeling of mine

about writing down prayers. She said, "Recently when I wrote down for the first time on paper 'I love You, Father,' it had never been more meaningful. It's a completely different feeling from list-making."

The first thing I ever happened to write (as I say, I just fell into this) was "I offer You my joy as a personal sacrifice. Whether I feel like it or not, before You continually I will rejoice."

It felt so good, I kept going: "Bless Ray: show him how to direct cantankerous people [there really are not many; what a wonderful flock! But in every group of people you have a few]—what to say and do, how responsible to feel. Give him guidance in Your perfect, highest will for his life. Keep him growing."

I went on to pray for Nels: "Give him a sense of responsibility. Help him to bring home Spelling Unit 24 today. [In the margin I wrote later, "Thank You, Father!" He did.] Help Ray and me to give him enough attention, not just playing with him but talking to him, listening to him, and teaching."

Well, if you could peruse as I do the pages of more than two years' worth of prayers, you would catch me in every mood of my life:

Praise You, Lord! This beautiful Sunday morning is Happy Day at Lake Avenue Church—worship day, fellowship day. May there be crowds flowing onto the campus all day to honor You together.

Father, give me a heart that gives really joyously. Help me to join Ray in giving recklessly! Make us ever more sensitive to the material needs of those about us. Father, is it asking too much that after we've done this, and as we continue to give, You might pour back to us enough to fix the house, too?

[Concerning Ray] Father, You are helping put our hearts

together. It's not easy. Thank You that we love each other so hard that hurts really hurt.

Father, I adore You, lay my life before you; how I love You!

O God! Have You left us to wander on our own?

Dear Lord, I need music! I feel so dry.

Father, it's a cold Thursday, a study day. Ray and I are studying in front of the fire. How wonderful! Lord, fill us with You today.

Lord, how the human element must be sanctified! O God, the cross, the cross! Help me to hide there again and again!

Father, I come to You about money. We're in a squeeze right now.

Dear Lord! It's so good to write to You again. I ran out of paper in South America.

Oh, Father, Hosea 12:6 is too much: "Always be expecting much from him, your God" (TLB).

Dear Lord, George and Joan need a buyer for their property.

Thank You, omnipotent God of all, for being my Friend.

Father, I love You so much.

Whatever it is, I spread out my heart before him. (Sometimes I laugh later at the dumb things I asked him for, which he was wise enough not to give me. I'm glad he has the final signature or veto. When I was a little girl I couldn't understand why sometimes my mother said "no," like the time when I heard that if your initials spelled a word you'd always have good luck. For several weeks I begged Mother to change my name from Elizabeth Anne Sweet to Elizabeth Anne *Ramona* Sweet, so that my initials would spell *ears.*)

Maybe you wondered at the first of the chapter why the "to do" idea can't be a tiny notebook to slip in your purse, why a whole notebook has to be toted around. Because the whole notebook is to be used continually, not just the calendar section.

You're waiting for an appointment to show up; use the time by browsing through the names of those in your small groups. Pray for them so continuously in the odd moments of your day that they become part of your bones.

You're on lunch break from work, and you have ten extra minutes. Flip to the "prayers" section, and just write to your heavenly Father whatever's on your mind. Tell him all about it.

You're dressed to go out, and you have five extra minutes. Peruse your "sermons" or "Bible study" sections, to refresh your mind about what you're learning.

You're stopped at a stop light! Flip open to the "goals" section; whatever goal hits your eye, you have something to mull over and pray about as you start up again on the green light, something you really long to be, or do.

As your notebook is filled with that which is most meaningful in every area of your total life, and as you learn to use it continuously through each day, you'll:

1. Stay on target in your living;
2. Become more prayerful;
3. Be more deeply impressed by God's truths;
4. Keep your mind filled with the pure, the beautiful;
5. Not forget what you're supposed to do!

When I was a girl growing up riding horses on Army posts, I learned that no jumping horse ever really wants to jump. No matter how pedigreed he is, if possible he'll turn aside at the last minute and let the rider go over the jump alone! So there's a crucial moment when spurs, knees, and hands tell the horse, "You're going to jump, and you're going to jump *now*."

All through the years I had fleeting thoughts of wonderful things to be or do. Or I had moments of actual conviction that I really ought to be this or do that. But somehow I let the moment pass.

I think of all the years I've believed in a daily quiet time, practiced a daily quiet time, taught others the value of a daily quiet time. But when a particular morning comes along with a long list of things to do, I'm just as tempted as anyone else to let it slip—just this one morning.

Then I need a sudden pressure—the equivalent of spurs, knees, and hands—that says, "You're going to meet the Lord first, and you're going to meet him *now*."

That pressure is my notebook.

13. Your Reaction to What You've Read

"Thanks for the book," you're saying, "but it's too much. I couldn't do all that."

Why? Let's talk about it. You may have legitimate reasons, or maybe not.

"Well," you say, "I've just never been an organized person."

Dear feminine friend, neither was I. Ask Ray. But as life's pressures and responsibilities began to get to me, I groped around for solutions. Shaping up to the three priorities has been the most basic help—learning to live with God first, from the inside out. The tools to accomplish this—my notebook, desk, closet—came along as a result.

Actually, I'm still not organized. But my notebook is, and I live by my notebook!

"But here I sit," you say, "with a girdle in the middle of the floor, dishes in the sink, and unanswered mail strewn on the bed. Where do I start?"

Start with God. Shut your eyes to the mess, or go for a walk. Humbly surrender your heart to his control. If you haven't before, let Jesus Christ his Son totally forgive you and wash away all your inner mess—of which the outer mess is just a reflection. Get washed clean, "squeaky-clean," holy and pure as only God can make you. Invite him to live at the very center of you, the control center.

(No, don't struggle intellectually over the legitimacy of conversion, as if it were a simplistic answer. God's order is first crisis, then process. Surrender to his crisis!)

You've done that? Then bite off bits and pieces of this book. Allow time to think through what week you'll work on this, what month you'll shape up that. I'm doing the same thing! He's not through with me, either.

"No," you say. "You don't see my problem. If I lived alone, I'd be free to do all these things, but there are other human beings within my walls. . . ."

You're right. And Philippians 2:1–16 talks about submitting and adjusting and being patient to reach goals the lowly way.

Your problem is probably temporary. Babies aren't organized, but they aren't babies long. Do the best you can. Children aren't usually organized; well, they leave you soon. Balance your goals for orderliness with a sense of humor. A husband isn't always organized, but statistics show you may not always have him to put up with. Adjust—and have yourself a great romance in these tender years. Roommates can be a problem. So you can change roommates, or decide the problems can be overcome.

But remember, for all your adult life you'll be a woman. And how you live your life as a woman, all by yourself before God, is what makes the real you. Nothing on the exterior can touch or change that precious inner sanctuary—your heart, his dwelling place—unless you let it. And God, who loves you very much, has tailor made all your outer life— your circumstances, your relationships—to pressure you into becoming that beautiful woman he's planned for you to be.

How much of his planning will you accept? You have a powerful God, and your expectations for yourself should be enormous!

Let me tell you a story that illustrates the difference high expectation can make. Do you remember the widow in 2 Kings 4 who had a big debt to pay, and got the news that her creditor was going to take her two sons to be slaves as payment of the debt?

The poor woman was beside herself, and she cried to Elisha, the man of God. His answer was, "Go borrow from your neighbors every container for oil that you can get. Don't borrow just a few. Really get out there and round them up!"

The woman borrowed containers from her neighbors. She poured and she poured, drawing from her scanty little supply. She poured, and when all the containers were full, she said to her son, "Bring me another one."

"That's all we have," he said — and with that the oil stopped.

Now, the oil poured so far was enough to sell and completely pay her debt, and keep her and her sons for life, as well.

Talk about a godsend!

But it was up to the woman how literally she took Elisha's instructions to get lots of containers. If she had taken his words even more seriously, she could have tramped over the countryside and rounded up thousands of pots! The oil would have filled them all, and the rest of her life she could have fed the other poor, donated huge sums to the temple, lived in a larger house, given her sons every educational advantage. . . .

Her expectation-level of God's ability to provide determined the quality of her lifestyle, forever afterward.

Lift up your eyes. Your heavenly Father waits to bless you in inconceivable ways to make your life what you never dreamed it could be.

How many containers will you put out?

14. What Is a Beautiful Woman?

How can a set-up of goals, a daily schedule, a notebook, etc., turn an ordinary woman into a beautiful one?

Well, what is a beautiful woman? Only once does the Bible say it just like that: "beautiful woman." The words referred to Sarah, Abraham's wife, in Genesis 12:11, and literally they mean "a woman of beautiful appearance." We know that she was still alluring to men at the age of ninety; she was some woman, physically! And yet she laughed at God's words in disbelief and then lied, denying it. And she was jealous of her maid. So physical beauty can't be everything.

In fact, when Proverbs 31 describes an admirable woman, her good qualities seem to be in opposition to physical beauty: "Charm is deceitful, and beauty is vain, but a woman who fears the Lord, she shall be praised" (Prov. 31:30). (Like the two fellows who were talking about their girl friends, and one said, "My girl has a great personality." And the other said, "Yeah, my girl's ugly, too.")

But the New Testament seems to put it all together by suggesting that the godly woman gives an *illusion* of outward beauty:

Let not your adornment be external only—braiding the hair, and wearing gold jewelry, and putting on dresses; but let it be the hidden person of the heart, with the imperishable quality of a gentle and quiet spirit, which is precious in the sight of God. For in this way in former times the holy women also, who hoped in God, used to adorn themselves" (1 Pet. 3:3–5).

Notice the word "adorn," which implies outer appearance.

Now, it's interesting that some Christians have stressed the submission of wives as if there was nothing else of significance in the Bible; but the fact remains that here in this section we find it used as the measurable test of a woman's gentle and quiet spirit: ". . . in this way in former times holy women . . . used to adorn themselves, *being submissive to their own husbands.*"

Whether we like it or not, these are the words of Scripture, in black and white; there follows a verse which redeems Sarah, with all her problems of disbelief and jealousy: she "obeyed Abraham, calling him lord," and for this reason she qualified as a beautiful woman.

"Never mind the features and figure you were born with," says 1 Peter. "What will adorn you with an illusion of beauty is a meek and quiet spirit, which is precious in the sight of God."

In other words, the beautiful woman is disciplined, chaste, discreet, deferring, gracious, controlled, "together." This kind of woman God considers godly, which means she's got his qualities, and she's close to his heart. This is "*his* kind of woman"—his kind of beautiful woman.

Now, under this umbrella of characteristics, she can have all kinds of personalities and still be beautiful. She can be vivacious or shy, colorful or cool, an administrator or a follower. She can be a corporation president or she can bake delicious molasses cookies—or both.

When a woman has God's beauty—a meek and quiet

spirit—she isn't threatening to those around her. She doesn't compete; she doesn't "demand her rights," because she's secure. Her trust is in God to exalt her in his own way and time, and he does! He can afford to expand her gifts and increase her place in the world, because she's not grasping for it. That's God's kind of beautiful woman.

Realize how this was true in Jesus' day. The culture of his day was a Roman, pagan, woman-degrading culture. That didn't keep God from honoring the aged Anna, a beautiful woman, with the sight of the new-born Messiah. It didn't keep Jesus from healing Peter's mother-in-law or the woman who was hemorrhaging, or the Canaanite woman's daughter, or the woman who was bent double; or raising to life the synagogue official's daughter, or the son of the widow of Nain. It didn't keep him from freeing the woman caught in the act of adultery, or commending the woman who poured perfume over his feet, or calling attention to the widow who gave an offering of two copper coins, or engaging in a long, life-saving discussion with the Samaritan woman at the well.

It didn't keep Jesus from having some of God's beautiful women as some of his very best friends: Mary and Martha, Mary Magdalene, Joanne, Susanna, and others. Beautiful women were the closest to the cross when he died, and the first to see him when he came back to life.

In the days following, beautiful women were with the men in the upper room those ten days awaiting Pentecost. Dorcas, one of God's beautiful women, was so loved by everybody that when she died God let Peter raise her to life. John Mark's mother was hostess to gatherings of Christians, and Lydia kept Paul and company as houseguests. Aquila and Priscilla, as a married couple together, taught Apollos proper doctrine. (Priscilla must have had a meek and quiet spirit, or her advice would have been odious But the fact is, she was one of Paul's favorites—truly loved and strategic in spreading the gospel.)

Never think that meekness is weakness. Meekness is strength under control.

God's beautiful women have been used even in mass turnings that have affected whole nations and generations. If you're a woman reading this, one of my sisters in this Western culture, you're an important key to revival in our day. When Paul heard the call to come to Europe for the first time and preach the gospel there, he traveled to Philippi, a key center, and found his way to a group of key women holding a prayer meeting (Acts 16:13). From this small group Christianity spread out until the whole known world was affected by it.

Through the centuries, God's beautiful women with meek and quiet spirits have suffered hardships, rocked cradles, and —you know the rest.

God's longest description of his ideal woman, in Proverbs 31, ends with these words: "These good deeds of hers shall bring her honor and recognition from even the leaders of the nations" (Prov. 31:31, TLB). The woman described here works hard keeping her home and serving the needs of her family, running the household with her head, her hands, and her heart. But she's hardly a pure domestic; she is also in marketing and in real estate and in anything else she wants to put her hand to.

In recent years we have been obsessed with figuring out what a woman should be allowed to do. God says in his Word a woman can do anything; the point is not what she *does* but what she *is*. When a woman is wise, and full of kind words, and hard-working and conscientious, and helpful to her man if she has one, and deeply reverent in her love for God—in other words, if she is a beautiful woman with a meek and quiet spirit—she can do anything in this whole wide world, and the world will praise her for it.

But with all this God-given, legitimate power, how do we as women influence the world for God? By influencing our

personal worlds to him. And how do we do that? By returning to him first ourselves, with all our hearts. Will it be easy?
Of course not. The worthwhile, the best, never is. It will
include disciplines—daily disciplines, to change us and
change those around us.

If you're a housewife with little ones underfoot, don't
chafe! This is not only their training ground, it's yours.
David, when he was young, cared for little ones too, sheep
and lambs. How could he go straight from sheep tending
into the king's palace, playing and singing his original com-
positions and influencing the highest power of the land? Because he was a self-starter, and while he'd been tending his
sheep he'd obviously been using his spare moments composing and practicing and developing his gift.

And take a deep look at those little ones of yours. They're
far more challenging than sheep! Only God knows what
they'll become when you're giving them Spirit-filled training
and love.

But whether mother or not, wife or not, you're a woman—
wonderful, unique. And even if you're paralyzed from the
neck down, you can be God's beautiful woman. His Holy
Spirit within you can give you all the self-discipline you need
to focus your attention on him, not yourself, to adore him
for large chunks of time, to think on his attributes, to confess
your sins to him and experience all the ways which involve
life's "top priority," and which concern your central core, the
real you. You have every resource to become one of his beautiful women, and to be a great influence on those around you
and around the world.

The timing of your life is also unique. It was time for you
to read this book. Opportunity, they say, is like a horse. It
gallops up to you from nowhere, and pauses. Now it's time
to get on. If you don't, he'll soon be gone, and the clatter of
his hoofs will be heard dying away in the distance.

Yes, you're a woman—handmade by God to fulfill wonderful plans of his. Do you feel a time-release capsule exploding inside you, urging you to new interests, new opportunities, new horizons?

Is it total revolution for you?

Write me and tell me about it.

Love,
Anne Ortlund
c/o Renewal Ministries
4500 Campus Dr., Suite 662
Newport Beach, CA 92660

For information on "Beautiful Woman" seminars write Anne Ortlund at the address provided above.

How to Use This Book

The questions and exercises in this study guide are designed for individual study which will in turn lead to group interaction. Thus, they may be used either as a guide for individual meditation or group discussion. During your first group meeting we suggest that you set aside a few minutes at the outset in which individual group members introduce themselves and share a little about their personal pilgrimage of faith.

If possible, it is a good idea to rotate leadership responsibility among the group members. However, if one individual is particularly gifted as a discussion leader, elect or appoint that person to guide the discussions each week. Remember, the leader's responsibility is simply to guide the discussion and stimulate interaction. He or she should never dominate the proceedings. Rather, the leader should encourage all members of the group to participate, expressing their individual views. He or she should seek to keep the discussion on track, but encourage lively discussion.

If one of the purposes of your group meeting is to create a caring community, it is a good idea to set aside some time for sharing individual concerns and prayer for one another. This can take the form of both silent and spoken petitions and praise.

Study Guide

NOTE: Before your group begins studying this book, the leader may want to order "Disciplines" notebooks and calendar pages, and at least have the group begin to use them for taking notes, making shopping lists, etc. In chapter 14, "Your Notebook," Anne tells how using a notebook has tremendously helped her and countless other women to organize their lives. But she has found that the "right" sized notebooks and calendar pages are frequently difficult to find. So Anne now makes them available. Order by writing the Ortlunds at Renewal Ministries, 4500 Campus Dr., Suite 662, Newport Beach, CA 92660; or ask for a brochure.

Chapter 1: Your First Decision, and What Follows

1. Which kind of woman are you, the kind who usually "takes life as it comes" or one who, as a rule, thinks ahead and plans for the future? Answer the questions posed by Anne Ortlund on the first page of this chapter and share your answers with the group.

2. What does it mean to "lose your own soul"? In what sense are we "saved" by reaching out to Jesus Christ? From what were you (or do you need to be) saved? *For* what are you saved?

3. Anne speaks of her *thirst* for God and of a time when she wanted "more of God" in her life. What do you think she means by "more of God"?

4. If you had more of God in your life, how do you think your life would be different?

5. Does the word *discipline* bring positive or negative thoughts to your mind? Why?

6. Do you agree with Anne's statement that "the disciplines of life are what get you to where you want to go"? Why or why not?

Chapter 2: Reshaping Your Life to Three Priorities

1. What are your top three priorities in life? List your (honest) priorities, based on how you spend your time and what you think about most of the time.

2. Do you think it is realistically possible to put God first in your life? Describe what a typical day in your life might be like if God were your Number 1 priority.

3. Anne suggests four ways to come to know God. Which of these do you already practice? What changes would you have to make in order to practice all four?

4. Do you agree that we should go to church whether we "get anything out of it" or not? Why or why not?

5. What are the personal implications of Anne's statement that one's "true source of godly love, warmth, nourishment, and togetherness should come from the larger family, the eternal family"? Is this how you view your church? If not, what could you do to make this kind of relationship possible?

6. Anne lists her third priority as the needy people of the world. Who

are the needy people in your world? If they were your third priority, which of your gifts would you use to minister to them?

7. See how Jesus' heart reflects these same three priorities in his prayer in the Garden of Gethsemane to his Father: John 17:1–5, 6–19, 20–26. See how Jesus commands us to live by these three priorities: John 15:1–11, 12–17, 18–27. In what priority are you weak? In what are you strong? How can you adjust your life to better reflect his priorities for you?

Chapter 3: Your Attitude toward Work

1. What color do you think of when you think of your work? Draw a circle and divide your work into three categories, giving each the appropriate size of the pie based on the amount of time you spend in that activity. Now assign a color to each category by how you feel about it. Yellow = exuberant, excited, look forward to it, it's important to you; Red = it's tolerable, important, but not to you, a yawn; Brown = tense, you dread it, it exhausts you and gives nothing in return, you resent having to do it. Share your discoveries with the group.

2. Do you agree that work is God's plan for you or do you wish you didn't have to work? Why does Anne think that work is God's plan?

3. How does following the three priorities on page 39 affect your attitude toward your work?

4. What special gifts are you using in your work? What gifts do you wish you could use? What kind of job could you find or create that would use your gifts more of the time? What would you have to do or give up in order to make this change?

5. What do you feel God is leading you to do in regard to your work? Share this with the group or a friend and ask them to support you in

prayer and encouragement as you start taking steps to make this change.

PREPARATION FOR NEXT SESSION:
Before reading or discussing the next chapter, take an inventory of your closet. Notice Anne's list on page 47, but see that her next sentence says, "This may be an entirely different kind of wardrobe than you need." List the categories which *you* need, and count the number of items of clothing you have for each category.

Chapter 4: Your Looks

1. Do you agree with Anne when she says looks are important? How does her formula of spending 1/22 of her time on looks compare with yours?

2. What is your own philosophy regarding physical appearance?

3. CLOSET INVENTORY
   Categories of clothing for   Number of items
   your particular lifestyle (for   of clothing
   instance, dressy dresses,
   day pants with tops, etc.)

   _____   _____

   _____   _____

   _____   _____

   _____   _____

   _____   _____

   _____   _____

   _____   _____

Share your discoveries with the group.

4. If you were to follow Anne Ortlund's philosophy of "eliminate and concentrate," how would your wardrobe change?

Chapter 5: Your Goals

1. How do you view people who set definite goals for themselves? Compare them with those who "fly by the seats of their pants."

2. Has there been a time in your life when you wrote down your life purposes and life goals? Describe how you felt during this period. What did you accomplish?

3. If you currently have your own goals written down, would you be willing to share them with the group? (As Anne says, goals are personal and it would be understandable if you prefer to keep them to yourself.)

4. Review the three categories of goals Anne Ortlund sets for herself, pointing out the distinctions she makes between "life purposes," "life goals," and "one-year goals."

TO THE LEADER: Dreaming and goal setting cannot be done hastily. Therefore, try to allow at least 30 minutes to an hour for the next four exercises.

5. Take a clean sheet of paper and write down your own "life purpose(s)." Be sure to use verbs in your sentences. Otherwise, your thoughts will be vague.

6. Write down your "life goals" (what you hope to do before you die). Anne says to make them *specific* and *large*.

7. Write down your "one-year goals." Now, check to make sure that each one-year goal fits into your statement of life purpose and life

goals. If one does not, you need to either eliminate it or rewrite your life purpose and goals so that this goal fits.

8. If there is time, share your goals with your group.

Chapter 6: Your Daily Scheduling

1. How do you handle your daily scheduling? Do you use a calendar? "To Do" lists? A notebook? Or do you try to keep your schedule in your head? Are you happy with your system? Do you make maximum use of your minutes, as well as hours and days?

2. Why is it a bad habit to try to remember to do things instead of writing them down?

3. How much time do you think you "waste" each day due to inefficient scheduling? List the things you do that are time wasters.

4. Add to Anne's list on pages 65–66 the things you want to do when you're tempted to waste time.

5. Now, take three to five minutes to plan tomorrow. Check to see if each activity helps meet one of your "life goals." Share your schedule with the group and explain how it leads to the fulfillment of a goal.

Chapter 7: Your Growing Life

1. What "place" came into your mind when you were reading about Anne's private time with God? Do you have (or have you ever had) a special "place" where you regularly met God? Describe it.

2. How do you identify with Anne's comment that her husband, Ray, is not easily ruffled?

_____ Sounds like me most of the time.

_ ___ Sounds like me occasionally.

_____ I could be like that if only . . .

_____ Sounds impossible for me.

Explain your answer.

3. What books or articles have you read this year that represent your special interests? What have you read (or are you reading) to "feed your spirit"?

4. How do you study your Bible? Describe the plan that works best for you.

5. If you have not already done so, set a prayer and Bible study goal for this year. Share your goal with the group and plan to report to them on your progress, asking them for encouragement and support.

Chapter 8: Your Life Behind the Scenes

1. Do you agree that one's physical surroundings should be a reflection of God and one's inner self? Why or why not? How close is the organization and appearance of your home to how you view your inner self? _____They are the same. _____They are alike in places. _____They are not alike at all.

2. If your home is not representative of the real you, what keeps you from making it so?

3. Anne refers to God as "organization" and "spirit." What does she mean by these terms? Do you think it is possible to let your mind *dwell* on what is true, honorable, right, pure, lovely, etc. if one has several children at home? How?

4. What is the atmosphere in your house? Choose a number between 1 and 10 to describe the *typical* atmosphere in your home.

1	2	3	4	5	6	7	8	9	10
cheerful									gloomy
1	2	3	4	5	6	7	8	9	10
quiet									noisy
1	2	3	4	5	6	7	8	9	10
uplifting music								agitating music	
1	2	3	4	5	6	7	8	9	10
a refuge									a zoo

Tell the group which numbers you circled and share with them why you did. What do you want to change?

5. What have you decided to do about your wardrobe as a result of reading this chapter and chapter 4, "Your Looks"? Share your decisions with the group.

6. What have you decided to do about your beside table? Your bathroom counter? Your time with God? Share these decisions with the group.

Chapter 9: Your Closest Relationships

1. Take a moment to think of the people on whose lives you feel you have made a lasting mark. Write their names down, or if there are too many, try to think of approximately how many lives you have touched in a significant way.

2. What person has helped you the most as a growing Christian? Was your time with this person structured or unstructured? If you have had the experience of being discipled tell your group how your meetings were structured, comparing them with Anne's design.

3. Anne says that God "constructed us so that we're lonely unless we

have firm, deep fellowship with him and with other believers." Does your experience validate this belief? Explain your answer.

4. How do you think a person would know whether or not he or she is ready to disciple another person? What qualifications should a discipler have?

5. If you were to accept God's call to be a discipler, who would possibly be on your first list to disciple? Think of various ways you might propose the idea to them.

6. When would you be able to meet with this (these) person(s)? What steps would you need to take between now and then to prepare yourself?

Chapter 10: Your Public Life

1. Anne says there are two kinds of personalities in the world, those whose attitude says, "Here I am," and those who say, "There you are." Which kind are you? Give reasons for your answer.

2. Think of someone you know who has a "There you are" spirit. Describe this person.

3. Anne advises us to "look quality, think quality, talk quality," and to expose ourselves to quality. On a scale from one to ten, rate yourself by circling a number in each category.

Looks	1	2	3	4	5	6	7	8	9	10
Thoughts	1	2	3	4	5	6	7	8	9	10
Talk	1	2	3	4	5	6	7	8	9	10
Input	1	2	3	4	5	6	7	8	9	10

Now, tell why you selected each number.

4. What can you do to improve in each area?

5. Is your larger circle of friends as large as you would like it to be? Is it too large? How do you differentiate between intimate friends and your "public" friends?

6. Tell the group what you would like your "public" to see in you. What has to be worked on in order for this to be possible?

Chapter 11: Your Desk

1. What do you need to do to improve the efficiency of your desk and filing system? Write down quickly each step you need to take. If you do not even have a desk or filing system your steps may include:
(1) Go by office supply store to check styles and prices of desks and file cabinets.
(2) Talk to _____ about making a desk with a door and slabs.
(3) Clean up _____ room to make room for a desk and file. (Your "file" may be a box which holds Manila folders upright.)

2. Next, number your list in the order of which should come first, second, etc.

3. Share your list with the group and add or revise your plan as you hear new ideas from others.

NOTE: If your group is in agreement, you may want to make the next meeting a working session with each person organizing her own notebook.

Chapter 12: Your Notebook

1. Take a few minutes to review how Anne divides her notebook and what categories she uses.

2. List the sections you want in your notebook.

3. If you have decided to make this a working session, go ahead and let each person organize her own notebook. Make sure that more time is spent *doing* than talking.

Chapter 13: Your Reaction to What You've Read

1. Do you agree with Anne when she says that one's quality of lifestyle is determined by her expectation level of God's ability to provide? Why or why not?

2. If you were to raise your expectation level of God, how would you show it?

Chapter 14: What Is a Beautiful Woman?

1. Anne says that a beautiful woman is

> disciplined
> chaste
> discreet
> deferring
> gracious
> controlled
> "together"

Write your name on the left side of each word that now describes you. (Don't be overly modest.) Write your name on the right side of each word that you believe will describe you in the next few months. Tell the group why you expect to experience these changes.

2. Think about Anne's statement that "You have every resource to become one of [God's] beautiful women, and to be a great influence on those around you and around the world." What specific resources do you have to become a beautiful woman?

3. Do you feel "a time-release capsule exploding inside you, urging you to new interests, new opportunities, new horizons"? Tell the group about one new experience you will have this month.

4. Spend a few moments in prayer, lifting up to God the goals, plans, schedules, and new ideas you have had while reading this book. If you are studying the book in private, write your prayer—and put it in your notebook!